D0867925

Swing Trading as a Part Time Job

Swing Trading as a Part Time Job

Brett Brown

iUniverse, Inc.
New York   Bloomington

Swing Trading as a Part Time Job

Copyright © 2009 Brett Brown

All rights reserved. No part of this book may be used or reproduced by any means, graphic, electronic, or mechanical, including photocopying, recording, taping or by any information storage retrieval system without the written permission of the publisher except in the case of brief quotations embodied in critical articles and reviews.

iUniverse books may be ordered through booksellers or by contacting:

iUniverse
1663 Liberty Drive
Bloomington, IN 47403
www.iuniverse.com
1-800-Authors (1-800-288-4677)

Because of the dynamic nature of the Internet, any Web addresses or links contained in this book may have changed since publication and may no longer be valid. The views expressed in this work are solely those of the author and do not necessarily reflect the views of the publisher, and the publisher hereby disclaims any responsibility for them.

ISBN: 978-1-4401-5042-5 (sc)
ISBN: 978-1-4401-5043-2 (ebk)

Printed in the United States of America

iUniverse rev. date: 06/12/2009

Table of Contents

Introduction

I have always had a passion for the markets. I have read hundreds of books on the subject. I was averaging about a thousand dollars a year on books that covered everything from day trading to fundamental analysis. I always thought there was something better out there, "The Holy Grail".

Whenever I started to lose money I figured that the system I was trading didn't work. I spent thousands on different software packages. I have been to several seminars and listened to top traders talk. I always sat in the front row and made sure I got my share of questions in. I have chatted online with world class traders. I had such a passion for the markets I thought the perfect job would be a stock broker.

I went out and got a job as a Financial Advisor at a major brokerage firm. I was a stocks and commodities broker. I thought everything was just perfect. I soon came to realize that brokers were just glorified salespeople. I left that job after a year. The best part about that job was that I was a broker through 1998. It was an exciting time in the market. I was always into tech toys and had been on Prodigy, the first internet service since day one. When they upgraded our office computers to Windows, half the brokers in the office needed help placing trades. The internet was just coming to life. I had an education of a lifetime while working there. I learned firsthand things you could not learn from a book or in college. For instance; in order to trade by fundamentals, the fundamentals had to be facts not fiction. Facts are not always what you have to deal with. After cases like Enron and Worldcom we all know that now.

Over the years I also learned that there is no Holy Grail. I thought maybe I wasn't spending enough on a particular book to learn the real secrets. I purchased books in the $150 to $200 range. I still didn't find what I was looking for. I even read a friends book that he paid $1000 for. It was on day trading the S&P futures. I don't think it was worth the paper it was printed on.

I heard Linda Bradford Raschke, a trader that I greatly admire once say, "If you have one watch, you know what time it is. But if you have several watches and they are all saying something different, then you are not quite sure what time it is." This one statement alone sums up the writing of this manual. It is not the Holy Grail. Your basic swing setups have been printed in several books and called something different by every author. This manual is a composite of basic setups that work. It also goes into just as much detail telling you what not to do. Fancy indicators are not needed. Expensive software is not needed. This is not a book promoting a service. I can't think of anything worse than paying fifty bucks for a book just to find that you purchased an advertisement for a trader's service.

Over the years I have had several people ask me to teach them to trade. I point them in the direction of some free websites that I feel are over the top. They have much to offer for free teaching the basics of charting. I tell them to read through the links I sent and once you have a basic grasp of what technical analysis is then I will help you. Very few ever come back. It actually becomes quite insulting to think that they expect me to sit down with them once for a couple of hours and teach them everything there is to know about trading. With the amount of time I spent reading and studying the markets, I could have went to school and became a brain surgeon.

This manual will not start you at square one. I wrote this manual with the intention of helping the average person take that giant step from investor to trader. A basic understanding of what a bar chart is and basic technical analysis will be needed. It will also help the more experienced trader break any bad habits they might have.

There are many good books on trading but they are written for a person who can sit in front of a computer during market hours. The average person who works a full time job cannot always manage this. This manual is written for the doctors and nurses to the school bus drivers and construction workers who are looking to make extra income from the market while working a regular job.

Swing trading is the best part time job out there. It can be very rewarding both financially and mentally. You will be going up against some of the most brilliant minds out there and they are all trying to take your money. By sticking to a game plan outlined in this manual you can out maneuver the fund managers. The Titanic didn't sink because it hit an iceberg. It sunk because it was too big to get out of the way. Mutual funds are too big to jump in and out of the markets. This gives you the edge. The fact is 80-85 percent of mutual funds do not beat the S&P 500 index. As I write this the first quarter for 2009 has just closed. If you went back ten years to the close of the first quarter in 1999 the S&P is down 38 percent. Therefore, the odds are that anyone who got out of college and started a new job in early 1999 has lost money in their 401k.

You as a small trader looking to take just a little piece out of the market can out produce the buy and hold investors.

Writing this manual has also instilled in me a set of rules to trade by. By quantifying a trading plan helps one to not be their own worst enemy. All of the information I have outlined in this manual is not new to me yet I never sat down and made one set of guidelines to trade by. When you force yourself to look at a checklist prior to making a trade and then put it in writing why you are making the trade keeps one from placing spontaneous trades. It will also take the emotions of fear and greed out of the picture. It all comes down to a numbers game. Play by the rules and the odds will be in your favor.

Chapter 1

The Truth About Wall Street

I will never forget the day that I learned the truth about Wall Street. It caught me off guard like a left hook. I knew there were crooked people in the business but I had no idea as to what extent.

As a new broker to a major brokerage firm I was eager to learn everything I could about the business. When the closing bell rang on Friday I found myself wishing tomorrow was Monday so I could get back to the markets. It reminded me of when I was a small child waiting for Christmas morning.

Every Monday morning all the brokers would pile into the branch managers office to listen to the squawk box coming out of the New York office. Working in a Northern New Jersey office I had done my training in New York and had met the "voices" who regularly talked on the squawk box and were often seen on CNBC. They were highly respected people on Wall Street. The voice on the squawk box usually started with how the major averages finished the week. From there any articles of interest from Barron's were covered. Then the voice went on to cover upgrades and downgrades from our firm and other major firms. I always brought a pad with me to take notes. Then one day the voice said something that changed my outlook on the markets forever. It went something like this: "We are upgrading XYZ to a buy because the firm is holding a large position in that stock". I could not believe what I just heard. In other words, the firm wanted to dump the stock. As a new broker I was encouraged to make 400 plus cold calls a day and push stocks the firm had buy recommendations on. Now this was back in 1998 when there were buy, sell and hold recommendations. Not strong buys, market perform, etc. They could not give it a sell or hold rating and expect to get rid of the stock so they rated it a buy.

At the end of the meeting I quickly went to my desk and pulled up a chart on XYZ. There was not even a hint of this stock going up from my analysis of the chart.

I knew some fundamental analysts were just downright wrong sometimes. Some were just better than others. I knew analysts like a football fan knows the players and their stats. I paid attention to who knew what they were talking about. Now the game changes when the firm they work for starts telling them what to say.

It wouldn't be long before I would get hit with that left hook again. Another famous tech analyst of the times said that Amazon.com (AMZN) would go to $400. Now at the time AMZN was trading at $200. AMZN had not made a dime of profit at the time. Not that many dot coms did in 1998. Although AMZN was, and still is a great company it was a big joke at the time as far as its stock went. Its nickname was Amazon.org (dot org is reserved for non-profit organizations). Although the analyst was laughed at by the media, AMZN rocketed to $400 in less than a month. Later it was found that this prized analyst had made buy recommendations on stocks because the firm he worked for had help bring them public. Inter-office emails were later uncovered by the New York State Attorney General where the analyst called the stocks that he gave buy recommendations on pieces of s@#%. He settled without admitting or denying the allegations. He was banned from the securities industry for life.

Are all analyst and their firms crooked? Of course they aren't. That does not mean that the information given to the analyst is the truth. Enron, Worldcom and Bear Sterns are a few of the most widely publicized disasters.

Bear Sterns

Bear Sterns was founded in 1923 by Joseph Bear and Robert Sterns. The firm managed to survive the stock market crash of 1929 without having to lay off a single employee. Bear Sterns went public in 1985 and went on to become one of the largest global investment banking and securities firm.

It wasn't until the subprime mortgage crisis of 2007 that sent Bear Sterns into a tail spin. Could it have been lies and deceptions or just complete incompetence of key executives? Could these executives really be that much out of touch with the business they are getting paid an exorbitant amount of money to run? At this point it does not matter. The stock holders paid the ultimate price.

The Wall Street analysts also need to take some blame for their horrific work. People invest their life savings based on what these so called experts have to say.

The following timeline shows the collapse of Bear Sterns with the corresponding dates shown on the chart in figure 1.1. As you read the timeline and look at the corresponding chart, try to imagine yourself as a BSC stock holder who relies on what the CEO and analysis say about the company to make your decision.

December 14, 2006 - Bear Sterns posts record earnings. The stock closes at $159.96

January 12, 2007 - Bear Sterns closes at a record high of $171.51

June 14, 2007 - Bear Sterns reports second quarter profits down. The first decline in four quarters. The stock closes at $146.07

June 15, 2007 - The Wall Street Journal reports a hedge fund run by Bear Sterns is in trouble due to subprime mortgage investments. A second fund in trouble will soon follow. The stock closes at $150.09

August 1, 2007 - Two Bear Sterns hedge funds file for bankruptcy and a third has its assets frozen. The stock closes at $118.30

October 4, 2007 - Chief executive James Cayne makes a statement saying, "Most of our businesses are beginning to rebound". President Alan Schwartz makes a statement saying, "The market is in the very early stages of a recovery". The stock closes at $127.61

December 20, 2007 - Bear Sterns reports a fourth quarter loss. The first in the history of the firm. The stock closes at $91.42

December 28, 2007 - Chief executive James Cayne sells $15.4 million in stock.($89.01 per share) The stocks closes at $87.35

January 8, 2008 - James Cayne is replaced as CEO by Alan Schwartz. The stock closes at $71.17

January 15, 2008 - Lehman Brothers reiterates an Equal Weight on Bear Sterns and changes the target price from $117 to $110. The stock closes at $77.57

February 4, 2008 - Punk, Ziegel & Co. upgrades Bear Sterns from sell to market perform and keeps its price target at $67. The stock closes at $91.00

February 29, 2008 - Punk, Ziegel & Co. reiterates market perform and ups target price from $67 to $90.

Deutsche Securities reiterates hold and lowers its price target from $104 to $90. The stock closes at $79.86

March 11, 2008 - Punk, Ziegel & Co. lowers its price target from $90 to $45. The stock closes at $62.97

March 12, 2008 - CEO Alan Schwartz makes a statement on CNBC saying, "We don't see any pressure on our liquidity, let alone a liquidity crisis. We are in constant dialogue with all the major dealers, and I have not been made aware of anybody not taking our credit. None of the speculation is true." The stock closes at $61.58

March 14, 2008 - Bear Sterns releases a statement saying it has secured funding from JP Morgan backed by the Federal Reserve Bank. Bear Sterns goes on to say that: "its liquidity position had deteriorated in the previous 24 hours." The stock closes at $30.00

Oppenheimer downgrades Bear Sterns from perform to underperform.

March 16, 2008 - Sunday night JP Morgan buys Bear Stern for $236 million or $2 per share.

March 17, 2008 - Monday morning Bear Sterns opens at $3.17

If you listened to the Wall Street analysts that were still hyping the stock or the CEO who went on CNBC and swore that Bear Sterns did not have a liquidity problem only two days before the end, you lost money. You need to seek elsewhere for the truth. The truth can be found in the price action. There is an old expression on Wall Street that says, "The tape never lies". When the trend is down and prices are still falling, that means people are selling. In the case of Bear Sterns, big money was selling. Insiders from the CEO to the secretaries. There was large institutional selling. All this information was revealed in the price action. The first warning came at the end of February when BSC closed at $166. A head and shoulders pattern was made. Prices later fell through the neckline with a big gap to the down side. This is a sign of people selling with lower prices to follow.

Bear Stern is not the exception to the rule. Misinformation is not a rare item on Wall Street. Do you remember a company by the name of Enron? It does not matter if you only trade in blue chip stocks. Sticking to the NYSE and big cap stocks will not save you from the hype that is fed to the public. It's easy for the analyst and the media to look smart when you're in a bull market and everyone is saying "buy". When the markets turn and they will, it's amazing how long it takes for the Wall Street gurus to adjust their position on the market. After all, BSC actually got an upgrade just one month before JP Morgan offered to buy then for $2 a share.

It happens all the time. Most analysts are value investors. If a stock is trading at $100 per share and it falls to $90, they think it's a bargain. Then at $80 a share it must be even a bigger bargain. There is always that possibility that it can go to $40. It a case like Enron, it can go to zero.

Figure 1.1

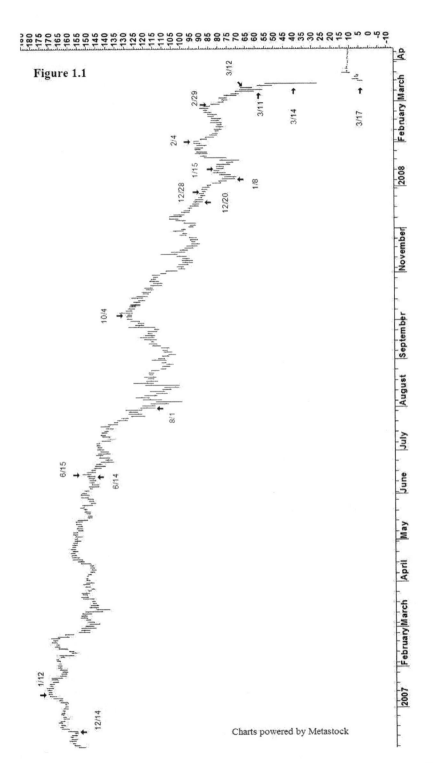

Charts powered by Metastock

Hype

If the market has a great day the media will give a good reason why it went up. Even if the market is having a great run and makes a technical pullback because it is overbought, the media will find a reason why it is down for the day. A technical bounce is not enough to sell the news. If you pay attention to the media you will notice that the market rarely goes up or down. It either "soars or plunges". If you got on an elevator and you had two choices, one button said "soars" and the other said "plunges" would you push either one?

Take little stock in what the media has to say. They need to sell the news. They always manage to find a bear to talk to on down days and a bull to interview on up days. Listen to what the charts have to say. Not people's opinions.

Chapter 2

Why Swing Trade?

In order to understand what swing trading is and why I trade this way we need to look at the extremes to show how we settle for somewhere in the middle.

Day Trading

Back in the mid 1990's I took a day off work to go to a SOES trading firm. I had visions of leaving my job and becoming a day trader. SOES stands for Small Order Execution System. The traders that traded this way were known as SOES Bandits. 1000 shares were the maximum shares allowed to trade. This was for NADAQ stocks only. Stocks were traded in 1/8ths back then. There were rooms with six to eight traders sitting around a table with one broker per room. Everyone had a computer in front of them. The broker had three monitors and three keyboards in front of her. I thought for sure they were all looking at one or five minute bars. Instead they were all looking at the bid/ask spread. Everyone had their own strategy, but for the most part they were looking for a quick blip in the spread so they could call out their order to the broker at the table. They were risking 1/8th to make 1/8th. That's 12 ½ cents! On 1000 shares, that's $125. The commissions were high. It was $25 per trade for the first six trades. That's $25 in, $25 out. The more trades you made, the cheaper the commissions got.

They all talked about how one trader at the firm who made one point in two minutes on a trade. I asked when that had happened and they said it was a few weeks ago. Based on the fact that there were about 35 people trading in the firm and one trader made a point and it was a big deal lead me to believe it didn't happen that often. I'm thinking the bandit was the brokerage house. With the birth of the internet and online trading the SOES houses are gone forever.

This quick in and out trading is called scalping. Traders look for very small profits and they make several trades a day. The only difference now is they trade at home with smaller commissions and they trade in pennies. This type of day trading keeps you glued to your computer. The only time they get up is for a bathroom run or to grab a bottle of antacid.

There is another style of day trading that is easier on your bladder and your nerves. You look to enter the market and you stay until your profit target is reached or you get stopped out. You get out at the close regardless of what happens. The most common entry is trading opening gaps. Most commonly gap reversals.

A true gap is when the open is higher than the prior bars high or lower than the prior bars low. There needs to be some daylight between the open and the prior bars high or low. It is not considered a true gap if the open is just higher or lower than the prior bars close. It must open outside of the prior days range. In figure 2.1 Flour (FLR) closed at $95.71 and its high was $95.85. The next day on July 2 FLR opened 53 cents above the prior days high at $96.38. It only traded higher by

7 cents to $96.45 before it reversed and headed lower. With a small gap like this, you would enter once the price entered the prior bars range. Once this happens, the odds are greater than 60 percent that the day will close in the opposite direction of the gap.

If this was a bigger gap, you would wait for it to trade up. Once Flour trades down below the opening price you would go short. In the example in figure 2.1, the stop would be above the day's high. Once you have a one percent gain, you can take half of your position off the table and trail a stop for the remaining position.

Figure 2.1

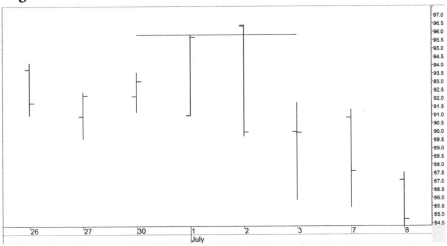

Charts powered by Metastock

Notice on 7/7 the open was higher than the prior bar's close, but it did not clear the high of the prior bar. This is not a true gap and it is not as predictable to trade.

Opening gap reversals can also be used to front run swing trades. In figure 2.2 Boeing (BA) was in a clear downtrend. Boeing pulled back to its 20 day EMA. A confirmation that the downtrend would resume would be when Boeing traded below the low of the pivot high bar at

$74.68. The next day, Boeing gapped higher and never even ticked up one cent. Once it penetrated the prior day's high of $77.21 by 20 cents or so, you could have sold Boeing short. You would have been in the trade one day earlier. That's an extra point you picked up plus a smaller stop above point **A**'s high.

Figure 2.2

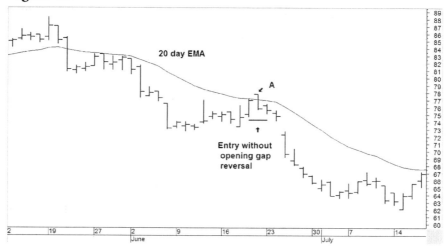

Charts powered by Metastock

Position Trading

There is an expression on Wall Street that says "the market takes the stairs up and the elevator down". Meaning the market falls much faster than it goes up. Months of gains in a stock can be taken out in less than a week. Position traders usually trade on the long side which eliminates profiting on down swings.

Position trades can last for several months providing you are right in your stock selection and entry. More homework is needed before the entry. Some fundamental analysis is done first. This can be very time consuming. The plus side is that day to day analysis is not needed. A 7 to 8 percent stop loss is used upon entry. A loose trailing stop is then used to keep you in the market until the market turns. A quick peek at the charts and the company news can be done on the weekend.

In figure 2.3 below is a chart of Walmart (WMT). On March 20, 2008 Walmart broke out of a three month trading range. After doing your homework on Walmart you decide to buy the breakout. You place your 8 percent stop in case things don't go as planned. In just a little over a month you are up 15 percent at the May high. You keep trailing your stop up to lock in your profits. Then Walmart makes a pullback. As an intermediate term trader you ride it out. The low is less than 7 percent off the high so you are still in the market. Things are looking pretty good as Walmart goes up to make a new high. You once again ride out the pullback just to find out that Walmart is again in a sideways consolidation pattern. In the last two and a half months Walmart has been going sideways. In nearly four months since you have been in the trade you are up less than 9 percent. This is actually a very good trade for a position trader. A 9 percent move in four months comes out to 27 percent on an annual basis.

Figure 2.3

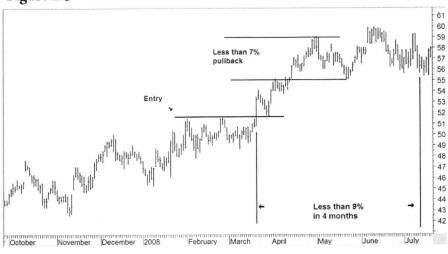

Charts powered by Metastock

Position trading is a great way to trade a retirement account. Short trades cannot be made in retirement accounts. There are also fewer commissions due to infrequent trading.

Swing Trading

Swing trades last anywhere from 2 to 15 days on average. It is a niche that the average person who works a fulltime job can trade. Unlike the day trader who never holds a position overnight in fear that the market will gap against them, the swing trader looks to capitalize on gaps and follow through moves. As a swing trader, you will look for stocks with momentum and capitalize on it. Holding a stock in a sideways pattern is dead money.

Because of the extra work involved in swing trading, a larger annualized profit is sought after than position traders. A swing trader looks to take small profits often.

Here are some bullet points on swing trading.

- Less stressful than day trading
- You can work full time while swing trading. Something day trading will not allow you to do
- Make money in up and down markets
- Catch short term moves that institutional investors can't trade
- Capable of much larger annual gains than position traders
- Catch a piece of the big moves and avoid sideways markets

Chapter 3

Options

Option Strategies

Option strategies are limited only to one's imagination. Strategies range from simple one legged trades like buying a put or a call to complex four legged strategies. Multi-legged strategies can be very complex and are beyond the scope of this book.

Vertical debit spreads are a favorite for many option traders. A spread is designed to lower the cost on expensive options. Some use the vertical spread to help with downside protection if they are wrong on the trade.

I personally don't like the use of spreads for swing trading for several reasons. One: if the volatility is that inflated (as it usually is a day or two before earnings) the trade can still fall apart if earnings are not as expected. Two: if you are right on the trade you just capped off your profits. There is no such thing as letting your profits run in spread trading.

Spread trades also don't work as one might expect them to. Let's say the underlying is trading at $100 and you enter into the 100/105 debit spread with 30 days until expiration. If the stock moves up 10 percent to $110 within the next few days, your maximum profit is $5. Now you don't see that $5 until you get closer to expiration 30 days from now. This fact often causes spread traders to hold onto the position longer hoping to see the full $5 profit. By doing so the stock can retrace causing what profits there are to erode.

What causes this is the fact that the short option's Delta increases at a faster pace on a percentage basis. At the time the trade is placed the 100 strike At The Money (ATM) option has a delta of approximately .50 and the 105 strike Out of The Money (OTM) option has a delta of approximately .25. So when the underlying moves to 105 the short option is now ATM with a delta of .50 or a 100 percent increase in the delta. The 100 strike long option's delta moved up to roughly .71 or 42 percent.

When you place a spread order and get filled at your debit price, you pay the ask price on the long option and the sell the short option at the bid. The stock could go up a point or two and the bull call spread could still be in the red when you go to sell. For short term swing trading, stick to buying calls and puts.

Options vs. Stocks

There are times to use options and times you should stick to trading stocks. If you are trading a stock listed on the NYSE that got beaten up so bad that it is trading in the single digits (as the financial stocks did in the early part of 2009), stick to trading the stock.

If the implied volatility is exceeding the historical volatility by a significant amount then you should stick to trading stocks. A good example would be just before earnings and the implied volatility gets so high making option premiums very rich. If earnings are as expected and the stock only rises a small amount, the implied volatility can implode. There is nothing more frustrating than being correct on the direction of a stock and still lose money.

If you are trading a stock looking to pick up a few points in the middle of a trading range, then you should stick to trading the stock. Even if you are able to split the bid and the ask on the way in, it is hard to get out with a limit order. Especially if you are not in front of a computer when it's time to cash in. If a stock is trading in a 5 point range and you are looking to pick up 3 points out of the middle, the ATM options with a delta of approximately .50 would move about 1.5 points. Depending on the liquidity of the option you can easily give up a half point between the entry and the exit. The alternative would be to trade deep ITM options. Three strikes ITM would give you a delta close to one. Deep ITM options can have less liquidity than the ATM options.

If the open interest in the ATM options is very low and the spreads between the bid and the ask are very wide then you should stick to the stock. Even stocks listed on the NYSE can have a 30 percent difference between the bid and the ask. You would need a substantial move just to break even.

When a stock makes a textbook 3-5 day pullback is the perfect time to use options. Especially if a new up trend has started and is running strong (ADX above 30). By the third down day the option premiums start to fall at a faster rate as buyers of the stock get nervous. Depending upon market conditions the option can almost double by the time the old high is reached. This will allow you to bank half of the position. The remaining position can easily become a triple.

On a gap-pause trade (covered in chapter 5), the option still has the volatility built into the premium. The spread will widen on a gap. If the underlying stock pauses for a day or two the spread will narrow some but the volatility is still present. Once the stock starts to move again you will find yourself paying up for the options. Front running the trade will give you a chance to split the bid and the ask on the entry.

Waiting for confirmation when trading options on a volatile stock can be a trade off. You have a better chance of the trade working but you have to put more of the option premium at risk. The spread will widen costing you more to get in. This extra cost will lessen the "wiggle room" you need to let the trade work. This is a judgment call and overall market conditions should be considered.

Keep it Simple

Here is a summation of rules to follow when using options.

- Stick to buying calls or puts
  ○ Covered calls and spreads are not for swing trading
- Have at least 30 days until expiration
- Buy ATM options
  ○ A strike or two out of the money is allowed on high priced stocks as long as it is not more than 10 percent
- Don't buy options if the spread is too high
- Don't buy options with thin volume or low open interest
- Don't use options on low priced stocks
  ○ Options on single digit stocks can double on a very small price move. You can also lose 50 percent or more on a small move against you
- Always use a stop as you would trading the underlying stock
- Never over leverage

Chapter 4

Getting Started

Trade as a Business

Your trading should be looked at and treated as a business. A computer in the family room will not cut it. A mail order business selling widgets for $3 apiece could not be run in the same room with your kids and their friends playing video games. You cannot run any home business this way. You need a quiet place to review your charts on a daily basis. Order entries cannot be made with interruptions.

You need a quality computer with a broadband connection. Many online brokers offer quality Java based trading platforms. They need a great deal of bandwidth. Although it is not necessary, I prefer dual monitors. This is an invaluable tool. You can keep charts on one monitor while the other has your trading platform. You can check earnings dates on the web before placing trades. Flipping back and forth from one screen to another can be distracting. Once you use dual monitors, you can never go back to a single monitor.

You need to keep track of all your expenditures. If you stick to the rules and you come out ahead for the year you will have capital gains tax to pay. You will have expenses and accurate records will make your life easier at tax time.

Software and Services

As a swing trader you will not need access to a real time quote vendor. Real time quotes and news servers can get quite expensive. The real time quotes and news supplied by your broker are more than adequate.

There are many paid services available. There are services covering everything from news, short interest and insider trading. Some services give trade recommendations. I believe you should educate yourself and play your own hand.

I have tried many services. Some are not bad on an annual basis. A service might offer you several trades a night. One or two might be winners. So if you only take a trade or two of theirs you might have a 50/50 shot of picking one of their winning trades. I always seemed to do worse whenever I was using a service.

Some of the services I tried were from top traders and the services were hundreds of dollars a month. I remember one option trading service I tried from a couple of high profile option traders. I figured I would give the service a try and see how their methodology compared to mine. In the first month every trade was a loser. How hard is it to do better than that on your own?

Another service I tried did have some winners. He claimed to be up over 100 percent in a 15 month period. He stated that you should never risk more than 2 percent on any trade. All trades recommendations and position sizes were based on trading a $30,000 account. Within a few days of taking the service he came out with a recommendation in Google (GOOG). He told you how many calls to buy at what price based on the $30,000 account. The total came to $28,000 and there wasn't a stop on the trade. I emailed him asking how can you state that you should never risk more than 2 percent and then come out with a recommendation to buy $28,000 worth of front month calls for a $30,000 account? His answer was that if he stuck to the 2 percent rule his model portfolio would only be up about 10 percent. He went on to tell me that performance sells and nobody would subscribe to a service that advertized that it was up 10 percent a year. As far as the stop went, he said he would send out an intraday email if he thought the trade should be exited. So in other words, it was all lies.

If you are going to try a service you should ask for a free trial. A week or two is long enough to see if their service is on the level. Also ask to see a performance record for their model portfolio. If they don't keep a model then ask to see their archives. Anyone worth their salt should have nothing to hide.

Data

Whatever software you decide on you will be in need of end of day data (EOD). EOD data is a fraction of the cost of real time data. It is usually ready to download about 20 minutes after the market closes. Even though your broker offers free charts and there are numerous charts available for free online, you need software to scan for certain criteria. The software needs a data vendor. I personally use Telechart[1]. Their data is very accurate and it downloads fast. The best part about Telechart is that their software has some great features. You can sort between specified dates. This allows you to sort between a recent low to the current date to see what stocks or sectors are doing the best on a percentage basis. You can sort year to date just the S&P 500 stocks

---

1   Copyrighted by Worden Brothers Inc.

to see the best performers. Then you can break the top performers down and look at that industry or the sub-industry. The program allows you to flag stocks that you might want to keep an eye on. Later you can flip through the charts by hitting the space bar. When you get better at spotting trade setups you can flip through hundreds of charts in minutes.

The charts and indicator list in Telechart is bare bone. I don't use indicators in finalizing my decision on a trade but I use them to help scan for stocks to watch. There are several software packages out there that read Telechart data directly or allow you to convert it.

Software

On a daily basis Telechart's software package allows me to keep an eye on my positions and run down my hit list. For my weekend work I usually use a more powerful software package with some custom scans to save time. I would stay away from software packages with proprietary indicators that flash green when you should buy and red when it's time to sell. I know the advertisements say they work with documented trades. Remember in a raging bull market a dart will work just as good.

Picking a Broker

Online brokers have come a long way. Commissions are getting cheaper and they are offering more and more as far as real time trading platforms and services. You will be generating a lot of trades. Many brokers offer discounts that can be quite substantial over the course of a year. You might have to ask for it but it will be well worth it.

Here are a few things to look for when picking a broker:

- No fees
- Low commissions on stocks and options
  - Many brokers offer low cost commissions on stocks but they fall short on option trades
- Non-web based trading platform (Java)
  - Web based platforms are slow and looking at option chains and hourly charts even after market hours can be frustrating when you have to wait for pages to load
- Mobile trading platform
  - If you can't get to a computer during the day then you really need a broker with mobile access. Some brokers simply offer quotes and trading while others offer charts on PDAs
- Low margin rates
  - You will need a margin account to short stocks.
- Money market sweep
  - Not all brokers do this
- OCO orders, contingent orders for stocks and options
  - This is very important. You will need to place stop loss and profit taking orders. You will also need to buy and sell options based how the underlying stock is trading (contingent order)

The above list is the bare minimum to look for.

Here are a few more things that you might want to have:

- Paper trading account
    - To try out new ideas. I recommend paper trading options until you feel 100 percent comfortable before using real money
- Able to trade futures from the same account
    - Something you will not need for awhile.
- Ability to sell naked options
    - Some brokers have very high restrictions to sell naked options

Other than the paper trading account, you will not need the other services for some time. Trading futures and selling naked options require experience and a good know how before even thinking of sticking your toes into those waters.

Publications like Barron's rate these brokers. It would be worth while checking to see who is on top of the list. I also like to call customer service to see what kind of response I get. See what hours they keep and call a couple of times. I like to call right after the market opens. If you can't get a human to pick up on the third ring between 9:30 – 9:45 EST then you don't want that broker. If your internet connection goes down and you need to place a trade it's nice to know someone will pick up the phone when you have a problem. Beware, some brokers charge a big premium to trade by phone. Watch out for hidden fees.

Chapter 5

A Look at the Charts

Types of charts

Many books have been written on bar charts. Some are dedicated to candlesticks alone. There are numerous books on price patterns and others just on Fibonacci retracements. Although it is always a good idea to keep educating yourself and read all you can about technical analysis, for the scope of this manual, I will not get into price patterns. Although all examples in this book will be bar charts, candlestick charts can be used. After years of switching back and forth undecided as to what charts I liked better, I found that I can see the "big picture" better in the open, high, low, close charts. A very short term turning point will stick out better with candlestick charts. I think if I was day trading, I would use candlesticks. It's a personal preference that you will have to experiment with.

Identifying Trends

Before you can even think of placing a trade, you need to determine the trend direction. Forget about your favorite stock and how good the fundamentals are. Forget about trading a stock because you really like their new electronic gadget. A good company product does not equal a good stock. Just like good fundamentals means nothing to you as a trader. If the stock is in a bad sector, then it is fighting the current. It's like building a million dollar house in the bad part of town. It would be hard to sell.

An uptrend is defined as higher highs and higher lows. It's as simple as that. A quick look at a chart and you can figure out if the trend is up, down or sideways. The purpose of this manual is to help find stocks that are trending quickly and sort through them to determine the strength of the trend. Although it is possible to find stocks without using software and indicators to scan a database, it would take a great deal of time. Short term trading while working a full time job will require the use of software. Charts found on the internet will not cut it.

Moving averages

As a swing trader, I like to look at the 30 day exponential moving average (EMA). I like the way the exponential moving average reacts quicker to price action due to it putting a greater weight on more recent prices. If the 30 day EMA is sloping upward, you look to buy the chart. If it is sloping downward, you look to sell the chart. If it is moving sideways, you pass on the chart. It's that simple. All too often the general public sees a high flying stock pullback for what looks like a great buying opportunity. They jump in the first big up day only thinking about how they are going to spend their winnings. The stock goes up another day or two and then WHAM! The stock falls off a cliff.

Figure 5.1 is a daily chart on Borg Warner (BWA). BWA bottomed out in March and went parabolic by mid April. BWA found support at its upward sloping 200 day SMA. The general public thought it was a buying opportunity. BWA moved ten percent higher over the next few days. The perma-bulls thought the uptrend was back on track. What was actually happening was a short covering rally. The 30 day EMA had rolled over and was pointing down. Under no circumstances should you as a trader be looking to buy this chart. This is a shorting opportunity.

Figure 5.1

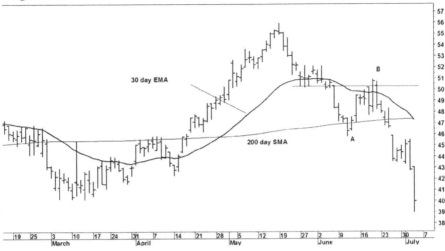

Charts powered by Metastock

Notice how the reaction low at point **A** was at the 200 day SMA. At this time the 30 day EMA had rolled over and was sloping down. At point **B** the rally back up to short term support (now resistance) was a bull trap. BWA rolled over and dropped over 21 percent in two weeks.

20 Day EMA

Once a trend is underway, prices should move well above their 20 day EMA (in the case of an uptrend, down trends are reversed). An orderly pullback to the 20 day EMA is one of the best setups there is. Notice I said an orderly pullback. If there is a big gap down somewhere between the pivot high and the 20 day EMA, it is best to flip past the chart and move on. The trade might work but why chance it? This is real money on the table. When it comes to your hard earned money, *you need all the ducks in a row.*

Price will often revisit its 20 day EMA as it stair-steps up. Trading off this can produce an excellent entry with a defined risk. More on this will be covered later in this chapter.

Figure 5.2 shows a textbook trade using the 20 day EMA.

Figure 5.2

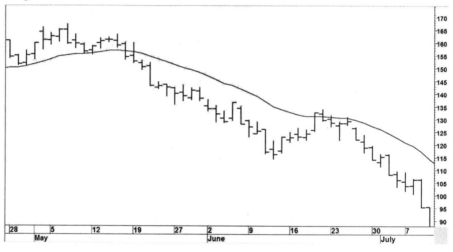

Charts powered by Metastock

Intercontinental Exchange (ICE) was in a clear down trend. A pullback to its 20 day EMA setup a low risk entry with a definitive stop.

10 Day SMA

Using the 10 day SMA will produce some of your quickest doublers. A simple moving average is used instead of an exponential moving average due to the short time frame. Strict money management must be used with setups using the 10 day SMA. Trading is a double edge sword. Fast profits can also mean fast losses.

The 10 day SMA is used in parabolic moves. When a stock breaks out, it doesn't always make an orderly pullback. If you wait for a pullback to the 20 day EMA, you will miss out on some very profitable trades. Parabolic moves sometimes never pullback to the 20 day EMA. If they do, the move can be 75 percent over. The downside is there is no clear stop. Using the 20 day EMA you can place a stop under the pivot low. This is too tight a stop to use with the 10 day SMA. Whether you are trading the underlying stock or the options, you need to use a dollar stop. Stops and money management will be covered in chapter 7. Figure 5.3 shows entries using the 10 day SMA.

Figure 5.3

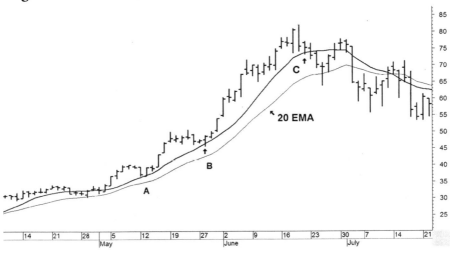

Charts powered by Metastock

Patriot Coal (PCX) had entries at point **A**, **B**, and **C**. There were good entries at point **A** and **B**. The entry at point **C** did not work but there were warning signs. The first sign was just the fact that by the time there was a pullback at point **C** PCX had a run of almost 300 percent in less than three months. Looking for an entry on such a shallow pullback after a run like that is unrealistic. The second sign was the fact that the 10 day SMA was just starting to rollover. Notice at point

A and **B**, the 10 day didn't even hesitate in its upward advance. If you had waited for PCX to pullback to the 20 EMA you would have missed the whole trade.

50 and 200 Day SMA

These two moving averages should not be ignored. They are widely looked at by institutional traders. It is the big money that makes the markets move. Most fund managers consider the trend down if price is below the 200 day SMA. Some not only need to see the price above the 200 day average to consider the trend up but they also need to see the slope of the 200 day SMA up. Price does not usually go through the 200 day moving average on the first try. That applies for crossing down or up. A clear penetration is usually accomplished on the second try.

Mutual funds also look at the 50 day SMA. They buy at the 50 day SMA or if they are looking at weekly charts, they look at the 10 week SMA (5x10=50). A stock in a long term uptrend will usually find support at the 50 day SMA. This is a sign big money is supporting the stock at this price.

Whatever their methodology is to enter the market, they refer to the 50 day SMA crossing above the 200 day SMA as "The Golden Cross". It is a bullish sign. Deep pullbacks to the 50 day SMA should be watched closely for institutional buying. Although not found very often, this is typically a safe entry.

Technical Indicators

There are software programs on the market that have over 100 indicators built into them. That doesn't count the fact that they have the ability to let you build your own. You are able to tweak and back test until you are blue in the face. Some have proprietary indicators. Some just give buy and sell signals using flashing green and red arrows on the screen. These programs can run from a few hundred dollars to thousands of dollars. Bottom line, you don't need any of it. Think about it. If these programs worked, then why would there be a need for hundreds of overpaid mutual fund managers? Anyone would be able to outperform the S&P 500.

Technical indicators are just tools. They are like a saw and a hammer are to a carpenter. The markets haven't changed. Don't buy or sell just because one line crossed another line in some fancy new indicator. For every chart you show me where an indicator gave you a profitable trade, I bet you I can find a chart where the same indicator produced a loss.

ADX

There is one technical indicator that I use more than any other for scanning the markets. Although it was designed to actually identify trades, I simply use it as a tool to help scan my database of stocks and industrial groups. It is the Average Directional Movement also known as the ADX. It was developed by Welles Wilder and introduced in his book, "New Concepts in Technical Trading Systems". The ADX measures the strength of a move but not its direction. A reading over 30 in the 14 day ADX represents a strong trend. A low reading is usually associated with a sideways market. A high reading of 50-60 is not necessarily better. When the reading gets that high, it means the trend has been underway for some time and a deeper pullback may be coming. A high reading is not however a sign to fade the market. Remember to trade only in the direction of least resistance.

If you pay attention to the slope of the trend along with the ADX reading, you will soon be able to identify a strong trend without the use of the ADX indicator plotted on your chart. It will always be an invaluable tool to use for sorting your database of stocks and industrial groups to show what stocks or sectors have the strongest trends.

Figure 5.4 shows the same chart of Patriot Coal (PCX) used in the example of the 10 day SMA. This time a 14 day ADX was plotted with a horizontal line at 30.

Figure5.4

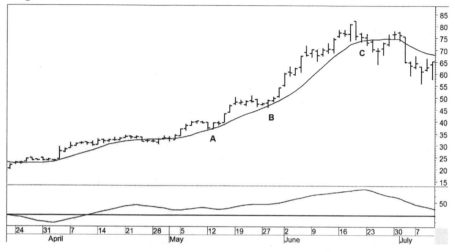

Charts powered by Metastock

The trade at point **A** has an ADX reading of 40 showing that the trend is strong. Point **B** has an ADX reading of 47. The trend is picking up momentum. At point **C** the ADX reading is 70. That is a very extreme value. The trend being exhausted from such a long run has come to an end. Down or sideways price action can be expected. Watching the stock at this point is just wasting valuable time. If the trend resumes or it turns into a confirmed downtrend, it will be picked up on our scans.

Most software can be scanned for stocks with an ADX above 30. Furthermore, you can break the list down even further by having two scans. One with and ADX above 30 and price greater than the 30 day EMA for when the overall market is telling you to go long and one with price below the 30 day EMA with the ADX greater than 30 for when the market is telling you to go short.

Figure 5.5

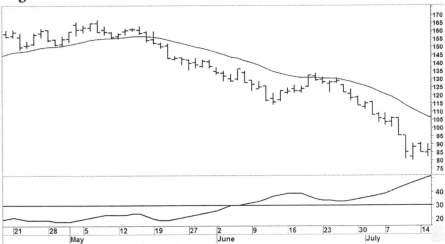

Charts powered by Metastock

Figure 5.5 is a chart of Intercontinental Exchange (ICE) with a 20 day EMA and the 14 day ADX plotted. Notice that the pullback to the 14 day EMA is the first pullback after the ADX crossed the horizontal line at 30. The first pullback after a reading of 30 is usually the best entry.

Fibonacci Retracements

Leonardo Fibonacci was a thirteenth century mathematician. It is said that Fibonacci discovered the relationship of what is now known as the Fibonacci numbers while studying the Great Pyramid. Each number is the sum of the two previous numbers.

The numbers are as follows: 1, 1, 2, 3, 5, 8, 13, 21, 34, 55, etc.

Any given number is approximately 1.618 times the preceding number and any given number is approximately .618 times the following number. The key Fibonacci ratios are: 0.0%, 23.6%, 38.2%, 50%, 61.8%, 100% and 161.8%.

Applying Fibonacci to Trading

I said in the beginning of this manual that the simpler the trading the better. How Fibonacci numbers came about is not important. Whole books have been written on the subject. The fact is that they work. Many opinions have been formed as to how they work in the stock market for timing and price projections. Probably because so many traders trade off of them is a better reason than any. I have yet to see a trading software package that cannot draw Fibonacci retracements. The percentages can be figured on any calculator.

Fibonacci lines are drawn between two extreme points. A peak (high) and a trough (low). If in an uptrend, you start at the trough and end at the peak. The retracement lines will project down with the peak being 0.0 and the trough being 100 percent. If in a downtrend, you start at the peak and end at the trough. The retracement lines will project upward with the trough being 0.0 and the peak being 100 percent.

The most common percentages to plot are: 38.2, 50, and 61.8. Most common pullbacks are the 38.2 percent and the 50 percent mark. The 61.8 percent line is usually a make or break line. If the 61.8 percent line does not hold, the move will usually retrace 100 percent. In major trends, deep pullbacks usually hit the 38.2 percent or the 50 percent mark and reverse in a single bar.

One must always remember that bar charts are just a scale of human emotions. A company's bottom line does not change from day to day. The low of a move is where there are more buyers than sellers and the high of a move is where there are more sellers than buyers. When the price on the chart hits the 50 percent Fibonacci retracement line (commonly called Fib lines), there are enough people out there that trade on fib retracements that the market stops fast and reverses direction.

Although Fibonacci lines can be used for projection of price, that is not as common and therefore not as reliable.

The chart in figure 5.6 of Nvidia (NVDA) bounced off the 38.2 percent retracement line and then went on to touch the 50 percent retracement line almost to the penny before going on to make new highs.

Figure 5.6

Charts powered by Metastock

Whenever a market makes a deep pullback, watch the 50 percent retracement line. It is by far the most watched. In the example of NVDA, an entry could have been made with a well defined risk at the $19 level.

The Setup
Breakouts vs. Pullbacks

There are two types of momentum traders, breakout traders and those who trade on pullbacks. There are arguments for both sides as to what type of trading is better. Breakout traders will tell you that you will miss out on some big moves if you wait for a pullback. Sometimes a

- 35 -

stock breaks out to either the upside or downside and never looks back. The negative side is that there are many false breakouts or "traps".

Figure 5.7

Charts powered by Metastock

Figure 5.7 shows a bear trap. MGM Mirage (MGM) tested support in early May at $65. Support failed and a breakout trader would have been short with a defined technical stop above support of $65. MGM lingered below support for several days until after hour news caused MGM to open at $79.69. That's over a 22 percent loss if you traded the underlying. When trading options, especially put options on breakouts, the premium skyrockets. I have actually gotten out of breakout trades a few days later with the price action of the underlying in my favor and I still lost money due to volatility drying up.

Figure 5.8

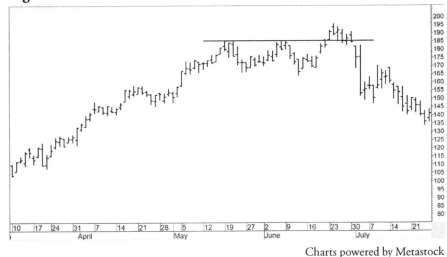

Charts powered by Metastock

A Failed Breakout can often lead to quick profits.

Figure 5.8 shows US Steel (X) breaking out from a two month sideways consolidation. The breakout was short lived and soon came right back in. A failed signal can be a strong signal in the opposite direction. If a breakout comes back in within 1-6 days, look to trade in the opposite direction. A stop should be placed above or below the pivot point. In the case of US Steel, a short trade could have been made with the gap down through the support/resistance line at $185. An entry in the low $180 range with a stop above the pivot high of $195 would have been an 8 percent stop. Because of the larger stop needed for this trade, position size should be cut in half. This would be an ideal trade for the use of put options. Because the stock is selling off from such high levels, extra staying power will give you the opportunity to capture a big move. US Steel dropped 17 percent in two trading days.

If there is a runaway bull market and a stock breaks out that is in a top sector, then it would be worth the risk to put on a small position. If there isn't a pullback, then you do not miss the trade altogether. If the stock makes a pullback, then you can add to your position if the trend continues.

Pullbacks

Trading on pullbacks is by far the most popular momentum trading there is. Some traders use special indicators. Others just look for stocks with an ADX over 30 and wait for a pullback to the 20 day EMA. If you had strict discipline and patience, you could make a living out of this one setup alone. Simply go long in up markets, short in down markets and sit on your hands in sideways markets. Limiting yourself to just one setup requires a great deal of patience. These setups are far and few between. When they do start to show up on your scans, they show up by the dozens. For that reason, I don't like to limit myself. There have been some great trades that I sat and watched go by while waiting for prices to come in closer to the 20 EMA. The stock will keep rising until finally there is a one day pullback. Hesitating to enter, I waited hoping there will be one or two more down days. Then I checked the market the next day to find the stock proceeded to climb without me.

Ideally you should look for at least two counter-trend days. In the case of a buy signal, the low of the second day should be a two day low. It is very common for professional traders to use a two bar stop.

Figure 5.9

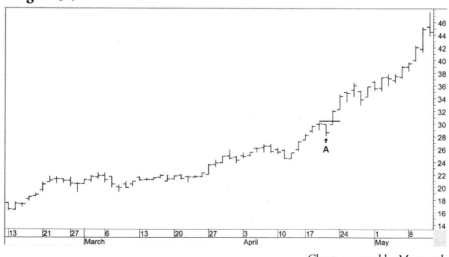

Charts powered by Metastock

In figure 5.9 the chart of Titanium Metals (TIE) shows at point **A** the low taking out the low of the two prior days. A buy stop placed above the high of the bar at point **A** would put you in the market at about the $30 level. TIE went on to make a $16 or 53 percent run over the next few weeks.

Following are some real life examples of actual trades and how they came about. The only thing missing from the equation is market and sector direction. All the trades were made using options. The exits were made based on overall market conditions. In unstable markets, sometimes it's best to just take what the market offers.

Figure 5.10

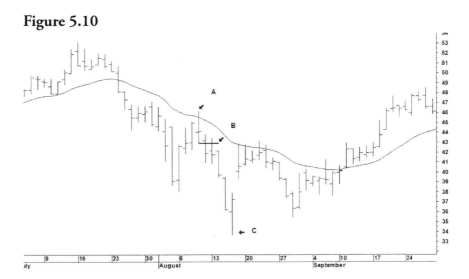

Charts powered by Metastock

Figure 5.10 shows a chart of Bankrate (RATE). In early August, the 30 day EMA rolled over signaling to only take short setups. At point **A** Bankrate's high hit the 30 day EMA and closed near its open. The next day at point **B** I went long the Nov 45 puts at a price of 6.70 when Bankrate fell below the prior days low. Four days later at point **C** the market was having a huge reversal day. An order was placed to exit and was filled at 12.00. The trade made a 79 percent profit less commissions all within five trading days.

Figure 5.11

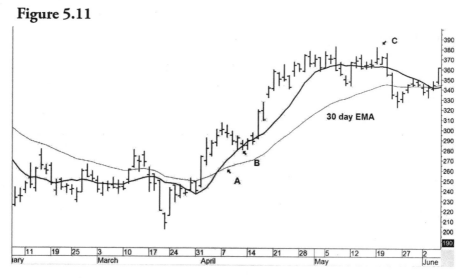

Charts powered by Metastock

Figure 5.11 shows Bidu.com's 30 day EMA (point **A**) turned up and the high broke above the March high. At point **B** I entered the market and went long the June 300 calls at 30.70. Because of the high premiums on the BIDU calls, I entered the market without confirmation. This is called front running. It was only done after BIDU pulled back to its 10 day SMA on a narrow range bar. It is a riskier trade without confirmation, but BIDU is a volatile stock and the premiums explode when the stock moves. At point **C** BIDU failed to make a higher high when the market was making a higher high. Momentum was slowing and I got out at 81.30 for a 165 percent profit.

Figure 5.12

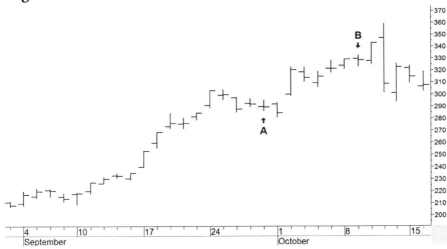

Charts powered by Metastock

Here is another front run trade in BIDU. After a parabolic run from $200 to $300, BIDU took a breather with some narrow range bars. On the fourth day I went long the Dec 330 calls at a price of 20.80 at point **A**. After one more rest day, BIDU gapped open and in seven trading days I exited at a price of 42.00 at point **B**. This was a little further out of the money than I normally would like to go. Sometimes on these high priced stocks you find a better value than the At The Money (ATM) options. You can go 10 percent Out of The Money (OTM) on high priced stocks as long as you have over 30 days until expiration.

Figure 5.13

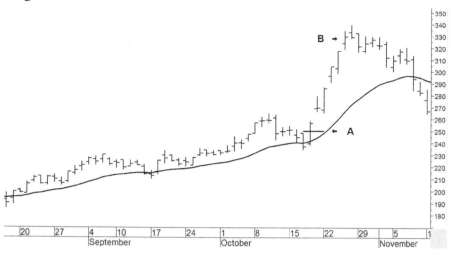

Charts powered by Metastock

On 10/18 Intuitive Surgical (ISRG) triggered a buy signal when it traded above the prior days high after pulling back to the 20 day EMA. Because earnings were to report after hours, it was a judgment call as to whether or not to enter the trade. The setup was there so I entered with a half position. I figured there might be a chance to add to the position if earnings were good. If there was bad news, I would only take a partial hit. The fact that it was October and I was trading the January options meant that the option still would have held three months worth of time value. The market was in an uptrend and so was ISRG. I went long at point **A** after ISRG traded above the prior days high. I was long the Jan 300 calls at 13.60. Five days later the calls were trading at 45 and I got out at point **B** on 10/25. That was a 230 percent profit in five days.

One of my favorite trades is a pullback after a breakout. You don't always get a second chance to get in at such a low level. It often brings swift profits and if the market itself is running strong in your favor, you can quickly bank half your position for a double and let the rest ride. If the move turns parabolic, you can use the two day low for a stop to take the rest of your position off the table.

Figure 5.14

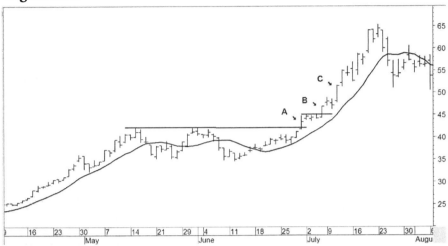

Charts powered by Metastock

In late June, Dry ships (DRYS) broke out from a six week base at point **A**. After trading sideways for three days, a buy stop was entered above the highs. Notice how the price never even came close to the 10 day SMA. On 7/5 at point **B**, I went long the Sep 45 calls at 4.00. Within three trading days I exited at point **C** on 7/11 at 8.00. Because the overall market had been trading sideways for the past few weeks, I took the whole position off. As it turned out, I had left most of the money on the table. In a not so great market, I considered a double four days into the trade a windfall profit. This wasn't an earnings play. It was just a price advance after a six week rest. The reason why it works is because other traders are looking at the same thing. The trick is not to be the last one in or the last one out. As a trader, you just need to take a piece out of the middle.

Breakaway and Parabolic Moves

The following trade is by far my most profitable trade. I call it the **Gap-Pause** trade. It usually follows earnings. Buying options before earnings is gambling more than trading. Option premiums can be quite high. Due to the volatility caused by the gap at the open, the spread between the bid and the ask can be too severe to enter. If you see a narrow range bar the next trading day, get your wallet out.

A one day pullback can be traded if it is followed by an above average move in price. Earnings are a perfect example. It is important to make note that the gap cannot be too big. A 5 percent gap is one thing. If the gap is too big check the news. It might be that there was an offer on the company. If this is the case, flip pass the chart and move on. The only exception to this is if the markets get so beaten down that once large cap stocks start trading at very low numbers as in the bear market that started in October 2007. Then a 5 percent move in a widely held stock trading in the single digits can be a daily thing.

The stock may gap the first day followed by one or two more up days. Then it may pullback for one day. In the case of a buy signal, you place a buy stop above the down days high. This will increase your odds as opposed to just jumping in. If you don't get filled the first day and you have a second down day, you keep moving your buy stop down just over that bars high. Don't do this for more than a few days. When it starts looking like a trap, stay away.

Figure 5.15

Charts powered by Metastock

- 44 -

In late October Google (GOOG) broke out of a base that lasted nearly five months (figure 5.15). On the third day at point **A** there was a one day pullback. Because it was also an inside day, a buy stop should have been placed above the prior bars high to avoid getting sucked into the market due to market noise. There was also a second entry at point **B**. By being a nimble trader and getting in at the first bar pullback let you get into the trade 40 points earlier.

Figure 5.16

Charts powered by Metastock

In mid June, Elan (ELN) gapped up through its prior high of $28 (figure 5.16). The next day was a down day. It was also an inside day. This is the type of setup you can front run. The fact that it is an inside day that closed close to the opening price is more important that the fact that it was a down day. A more conservative play would have been to wait for it to trade over the prior day's high. There is a tradeoff in waiting for confirmation. Often the stock will gap the next day or open and not look back. Either way the option premium will spike more than it already did from the prior day's gap. I like to enter this trade on the inside day just before the close if I am lucky enough to spot the setup. A stop can be placed below the gaps day low regardless of the dollar loss. If you get stopped out in the next day or two, it should be less than a 20 percent loss if you traded the calls as long as the option is liquid enough.

Figure 5.17

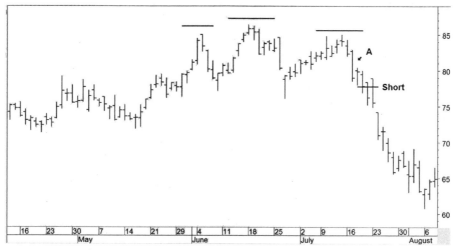

Charts powered by Metastock

In early June Sunoco (SUN) made a 52 week high (figure 5.17). The next higher high was made with one bar. The price came back in the very next bar showing a sign of a weakening stock. The next low was a lower low. The odds are against SUN making a new high. Point **A** shows a wide range bar down. This is over a 4 percent drop. The next day was the first up day. An order to sell short should be placed below the low of this bar.

The six month uptrend has come to an end and SUN lost over 20 percent over the next three weeks. The reason why momentum picked up on the downside was due to the price falling through the neckline on the head and shoulders pattern. The theory behind this pattern is that the public bought the new high in the middle of June (the head). When the price advance halted and came back in, the public was stuck with a loss. Unable to deal with a loss, the novice trader looks to get out at break even or close to it. The last attempt of a rally (right shoulder) was the late comers jumping ship. Once the neckline (support) was broken, SUN was in a freefall. In three weeks, SUN gave back everything it had gained in the last four months.

Chapter 6

A Glance at the Markets

Market Analysis

Jesse Livermore never used the term bullish or bearish when referring to the market trend. He felt that led to a mindset of a long term trend. He used the term, "line of least resistance." Livermore felt that by using the term uptrend or downtrend, it was much easier to accept a reversal in a trend than if you had a strong bullish or bearish bias.

Fundamentals and common sense may tell you one thing and the charts may tell you something else. Just like the second quarter of 2009 when the fundamentals pointed to lower prices in the XLF. Common sense should have told you that problems with the sub-prime mortgages didn't go away overnight. Still the XLF went on to rally over 60 percent. The trick is: **trade the market you see, not what you think will happen.**

A quick glance of the S&P chart in figure 6.1 may look like the market has put in its low and the market correction is over and the uptrend will resume. A closer look will show clues as to why this may not be the case and to hold off on establishing new long trades.

First we draw Fibonacci retracement lines from the October highs to the lows set in January and March. The May high came in at the 50 percent retracement level. A reversal off of this level would lead to the conclusion that the market could very well retest the January - March lows.

Figure 6.1

Charts powered by Metastock

Highs that fail to make new highs followed by lower lows are the first warning sign of a struggling market. This was just a counter-trend correction. This followed by a trend line break are a sure sign an uptrend has ended. At this point you are not sure if the trend will go sideways for some time before resuming its trend.

Figure 6.2 is a continuation chart of the S&P 500. You will notice the high made in late May did not take out the previous high (the 50 percent retracement level). That was soon followed by a lower low. At this point, the 10 day SMA has crossed below the 30 day EMA and the 30 day EMA is sloping down. Then the market rallies for three days to the 10 day SMA and stalls (point **A**). You should be looking to go short the next trading day.

Figure 6.2

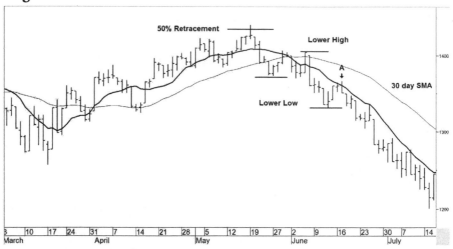

Charts powered by Metastock

That is not a green light to jump in and short anything. True the market has been in a downtrend since the highs made in October 2007. Some stocks have been putting in higher highs and lower lows since October. Shorting these stocks before their time would be detrimental to your account balance.

Now that you know the market is telling you to go short, you need to know what sectors to look to short. Just like in a bull market there are always leading sectors. When the market is in a correction, the weaker sectors should be focused on.

Sector Analysis

The S&P is made up of ten major sectors.

They are as follows:

Energy   Health Care
Materials   Financials
Industrials   Utilities
Consumer Discretionary   Telecom
Consumer Staples   Technology

Telechart[1] lets you divide the market into 31 industrial groups and 239 sub-industrial groups. To say the energy sector is in an uptrend only tells half the story. At the time of this writing, crude oil has been in a major uptrend, not all sub-industries in the energy market are heading in the same direction. While the drillers and the service companies have been following crude oil, the refiners are in a major down trend. In figure 6.3 you can see an overlay of the United States Oil Fund ETF (USO) vs. Tesoro (TSO), a major refiner. You need to break each industry group down into sub-industries before your final analysis.

Figure 6.3

Charts powered by Metastock

Sticking to the example in figure 6.2, after the market closes on June 16, 2007 we know we will be looking to go short the next day. You should already know from your weekend work which sectors are the leaders and which sectors are leading the market lower.

After comparing the sub-sectors to the S&P 500 index, Telechart lets you sort the values of the 239 sub-industry groups with the best performers at the top of the list with a score of 100 and the worst performers at the bottom of the list with a score of 0. It's that simple. You should look to short a stock in a sector at the bottom of the list. There should be at least a dozen sectors with a score of zero.

Figure 6.4 shows the Investment Brokerage-National sub industry group. Point **A** was the signal to go short the market on the chart of the S&P 500. Notice the 10 day SMA is pulling away from the 30 day EMA. As we learned in chapter 4, this is a sign the trend is getting stronger.

Figure 6.4

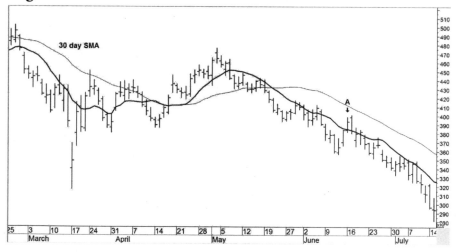

Charts powered by Metastock

The leading sub-industry groups should also be looked at for inflection points. Figure 6.5 shows a chart of the steel and iron sub-group. It has been one of the strongest sub-sectors year to date. In mid June when the S&P was flashing short signals, the steel and iron group was just starting to roll over. The 30 day EMA is just starting to turn down. Although this is not a signal to go short the steel and iron group, it is telling you that the stronger sectors are now starting to rollover. This market might take out the old lows set in March.

The commodity stocks can sometimes trade independently from the rest of the market. There can be a bull market in commodities when the rest of the market is going sideways. Energy, hard and soft commodity stocks can sometimes hold a market up or start it to rally. This is usually short lived. A closer look at what is actually moving the market will give you an insight of what's to come.

Figure6.5

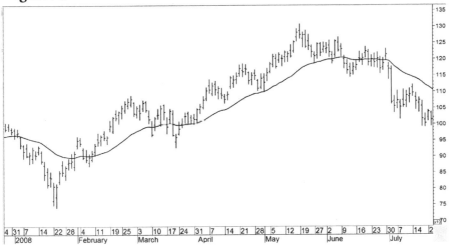

Charts powered by Metastock

Finally the Trade

We now know that the market is telling us to look for short setups. The Financials are one of the worst performing sectors in the market. Furthermore, the Investment Brokerage-National sub-industry group is one that can be looked at for potential trades. Figure 6.6 is a chart of Merrill Lynch (MER). Point **A** is the day we got the short signal in the S&P. MER rallied to the 10 day SMA. It was also old support which is now resistance. *Now all the ducks are in a row.* You cannot get better odds in your favor. The next day a stop order to sell short is placed below the low. We are in the market the next day. MER trades 30 percent lower over the next few weeks.

Figure 6.6

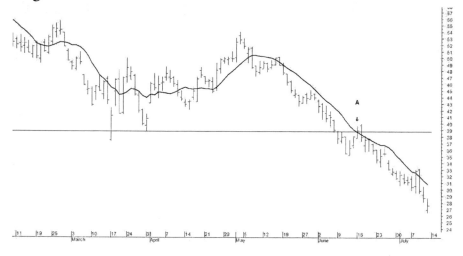

Charts powered by Metastock

Chapter 7

Money Management

Expect losses

Most people don't realize just what a 50 percent loss means to their account. If you have a $20,000 account and you lose 50 percent, your account value is now $10,000. That part is obvious. What people don't realize is that you need to make 100 percent on your money to get back to $20,000. A gain of 50 percent at this point only gets you back to $15,000. The math is simple but yet not obvious. When you consider that for a 46 year period from 1963 through 2008 the S&P 500 is up an average of 7.10 percent a year. You could spend years trying to get back to even. Controlling losses is the secret to success.

The Only Guarantee you will find in this Manual

Over the years I have tried different services and subscribed to different publications. Because of this I am on every spam list out there. I get more emails and snail mails of offers promising to "double your money" or "retire rich". One even said they "guarantee" to produce twelve winning options trades or your money back. I guess you could offer up one hundred trades and the odds will be in your favor of having twelve winners. It's all lies. Nobody can guarantee you anything except me. **I can guarantee you that if you do not place protective stop losses on every trade you will not make it as a trader.** There are no maybes or exceptions. A trader gets paid to take chances. You will not always be right. You may only be right half of the time. Keeping your losses small and letting your profits run is the secret to success as a trader.

Money Management for Options

There will be times when you win a few trades and lose a few. A dozen trades will go by and your account size will be near the same level as it was at the beginning of the month. You will become very disheartened and start to question your game plan.

Nobody and I mean nobody makes money day in and day out. People who trade their own account for a living to hedge fund managers expect losses. When you run into a series of several losses in a row it is time to go to cash and wait. Sitting on cash is a position. The market will soon show its hand and give you a clear picture. Preservation of capital is the key.

It's easy when there is a ripping bull market and everything you throw at the wall sticks. Everybody looks like a market guru then. A good friend of mine once told me, "Never confuse a strong bull market with being a great trader."

In your option trading account, you should never risk more than 50 percent on a trade. Ideally a 30 percent stop is better. This way if you get slammed with a bad fill on the way out, it will still keep you under the 50 percent mark.

Your position size should be a percent of your account. This way if the market is going against you and you have a few losing trades you will be initiating less money per trade. Conversely, if the wind is at your back you will be betting more as you should be.

Let's take a look at how money management can help even if you are wrong more times than you are right in your trading decisions.

If you started with a trading account of $20,000 and allocated 5 percent of your account per trade that would mean that your first trade would be $1,000. Figure 7.1 shows ten trades. Each trade is 5 percent of the account value. 40 percent of the trades were winners and 60 percent were losers. By limiting the losing trades to 30 - 50 percent and letting the winners ride, you can be wrong more times than right and still pull a profit. The example showed a gain of 12 percent profit over the 10 trades.

By the position size decreasing when you are on a losing streak keeps you in the game until the odds turn in your favor.

Figure 7.1

Trade Size	P/L	% P/L	Balance
$1,000	($400)	-40%	$19,600
$980	$980	100%	$20,580
$1,029	($309)	-30%	$20,271
$1,014	$1,521	150%	$21,792
$1,090	$872	80%	$22,664
$1,133	($567)	-50%	$22,097
$1,105	(332)	-30%	$21,765
$1,088	($326)	-30%	$21,439
$1,072	$1,289	120%	$22,725
$1,136	($341)	-30%	$22,384

When you first start out trading options I would suggest not allocating more than 20 percent of your account to option trades. Even then, I would only go that high if there was a clear and defined trend. Choppy markets will clean out a buyer of options. Even if the market moves in your favor slightly, the spreads are so wide that you could close the trade in the red.

Typically you would look for 100 percent profit on an option trade. Because not all months are traded on all stocks you sometimes have to go out further in time than a typical swing trader looks for. Some swing traders will argue that you should always use front month contracts as long as there is at least two weeks until expiration. That may very well work if you sit in front of a computer all day. If you work a full time job you may miss your exit. Typically six to eight weeks is ideal. This extra time will give the trade a chance to work and still have some time value if you are wrong. You can also take half your profits off the table on a double and use a trailing stop for the rest of the position.

Some of the higher price stocks have some big premiums. Smaller accounts will only be able to trade in single option contracts. It is still possible to take partial profits with a single option contract.

Figure 7.2

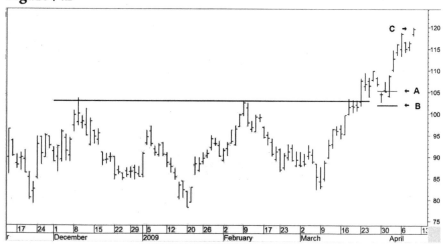

Charts powered by Metastock

Figure7.2 is a daily chart of Apple (AAPL). AAPL went sideways for over five months before breaking out to the upside. On March 30 AAPL gapped down after going sideways for four days. The fact that AAPL gapped down and closed down 5 percent is not a good sign. Because the low bounced off the support line (now resistance) and closed in the upper 25 percent of the day's range is a positive sign. The high of the day was $105.01. A buy stop could have been placed the next day at $105.30 (point **A**). A technical stop can be placed under the low at point **B** at $101.95. (Never use whole dollars or dimes for a stop. For example: instead of 50 cents, use 45 cents for a sell stop or 55 cents for a buy stop) On March 31 AAPL gapped open to $105.45 hitting our stop. The May 105 ATM call opened at 8.2. We are long one May 105 call at the cost of $820. At a delta of around .50 our technical stop should put us at a 20 percent loss if we are wrong. In the real world with a market order to dump the option at the bid will probably be more like a 30 percent loss. A technical stop that is within our dollar range is ideal. At point **C** AAPL closed at $119.57. Up $14.12 or 13.9 percent from our entry. The May 105 call closed at: bid 16.95 ask 17.07. That's over a 100 percent move in the option. Our profit target has been hit but there is still plenty of life in the option. Although AAPL looks a little overbought, it shows no sign of changing direction. Usually the longer the base the bigger the move.

We can roll the May 105 call into a May 120 call. The May 120 call closed at: bid 7.15 ask 7.20. This way we have half our money off the table and we are still long AAPL. Of course a trailing stop will still be required.

You need proper money management to be able to stay in the game when the market makes a big move. There will be times when you will be raking in money. You can double your money in a 10-20 percent move in the stock as we just saw in the AAPL example. Buying ATM options with less than 30 days of time value can double with a very small percentage move in the underlying stock. Of course this is a double edged sword. If the underlying stock goes against you for a few days the front month options are going to cost you more in commissions than you can sell them for. People who trade front month options usually bet the whole premium. Position size should be adjusted accordingly.

Money Management for Stocks

It is always better to use a technical stop than a dollar stop if you can. That goes for option trades as well as stock trades. A technical stop is a price that the stock should not return to once the original move is back underway. It should be above (short trade) or below (long trade) the pivot point. Sometimes the last bar in the pivot point has a wide range making a technical stop too large. At times like this, you need to use a dollar stop.

The actual dollar stop also depends on the volatility of the stock. A stock like Procter and Gamble (PG) is much less volatile than a high flying stock of the times. In the late 1990's it was tech stocks. In 2008 it was energy stocks.

Also watch out for low dollar stocks. Say you allocate $3000 per trade. If you find a stock that is trading at $3 that does not necessarily mean it's ok to buy 1000 shares. A 5 percent move in a $3 stock is only 15 cents. A $3 stock can move against you 50 cents and then turn and close up for the day. Bank of America (BAC) opened on February 20, 2009 at $3.61 and hit a low of $2.53 before climbing to $4.09 for the high of the day. That's over a 61 percent range in one day. Moves like that are not uncommon for low priced stocks. You need to adjust your position size accordingly. Try to keep your loses to 2 percent of your account. If you cannot, adjust your position size or pass on the trade if the stop needs to be that wide.

Here are some general guidelines for figuring position size and dollar risk per trade.

Account size x 2% = Account dollar risk

Stock price x 4% = Dollar risk per share

Account dollar risk / Dollar risk per share = Number of shares purchased

The above formula risks 2 percent of your account on a single trade. The actual dollar risk per share should be 4 – 5 percent. This will vary depending upon market conditions and the volatility of an individual stock. Too tight a stop and you can get whipsawed. When a larger percentage stop is needed then the shares per trade will be reduced.

Let's look at an example:

Account size = $20,000   Share price = $50

$20,000 x 2% = $200 total risk

$50 x 4% = $2.00 risk per share

$200 / $2.00 = 100 shares

Now let's look at a trade were you need to risk a higher percentage due to a more volatile stock:

Account size = $20,000   Share price = $20

$20,000 x 2% = $200 total risk

$20 x 6% = $1.20 risk per share

$200 / $1.20 = 166 shares

Because lower dollar stocks have wider percentage swings, you will need to risk a higher percentage per share. A $10 stock will need a $1.00 stop. That's a 10 percent stop. A $20 stock will need roughly a $1.50 stop.

Position size should always be based on your dollar risk of your account. There are many traders that will tell you to divide your account size by 10 and that is what you base your size on. In doing that you will be purchasing way too many shares of a lower priced stock and not enough shares of a higher priced stock.

Profit Targets

When trading options with four to six weeks until expiration you should look for a 100 percent profit target. This is not an unrealistic goal. The move in the underlying stock to double an ATM option with 30 days until expiration could be in the 10-15 percent range. An OTM option with 3 months until expiration will require a 15-20 percent advance in the underlying stock to double the option. Of course this all depends on market conditions and how long the advance takes.

Profit targets on stocks should be in the range of 7-9 percent. If you are risking 4 percent then your initial profit target should be in the 7 percent range. Lower priced stocks that require larger stop loses should also have greater profit targets. A 9 percent profit target is well within grasp. A 10 dollar stock with a $1.00 or 10 percent stop should have at least a $1.00 profit target. Never have a profit target less than your initial risk.

Although a lower priced stock can offer great upside potential, you can't expect a great risk/reward on the initial profit target. A $40 stock with a 4-5 percent risk can offer a greater risk/reward initially. Don't expect more than a one to one risk/reward ratio on a $10 stock.

When to Stay Out

To quote Jesse Livermore: "It's not the thinking that makes the money, it's the sitting". There are times when it's beneficial to stay out of the markets. You won't make any money but you won't lose any either. In Figure 7.3 is a chart of the S&P 500. The S&P has been in a down trend for over a year. Short trades have been the only trades that should have been taken. At point **A** the S&P made a new low after bouncing off the 30 day EMA. A five day advance brought the S&P up 19 percent. This was followed by a one day drop with no follow through to the down side (point **B**). Then the index went sideways and the 30 day EMA flat lined. Then in mid February support gave way and the S&P made a new low (point **C**). There was a shorting opportunity into the first week of March. By mid March the index was at resistance but the 30 day EMA was turning up (point **D**). New shorts should not be taken at this point. Any trades made from December to mid February while the 30 day EMA was moving sideways would have whipsawed your bottom line. Market makers don't have a crystal ball either. Without knowing their risk, they widen the spreads on options. A 30 percent spread between the bid and the ask is not unheard of in thinner traded options.

Figure 7.3

Charts powered by Metastock

It is also wise to stay out of the market when you have something going on in your life that takes time away from the market. Whether it is working extra overtime or planning a vacation. Get out of the market and wait until you can give your research your full attention. The market will always be there.

Chapter 8

Putting it all Together

Approach

I approach the market with a quasi-top down approach. I start at the top with the indexes and then run scans looking for securities. I meet somewhere in the middle. I don't look at work economics or charts on foreign markets. Looking at the S&P 500 and the NASDAQ Composite is enough to tell you if you should be long, short or out of the market. The media gives most of its attention to the Dow Jones 30. I don't put much weight in this index. Thirty stocks are not enough to get a feel for the general market. One stock has a bad day and the Dow can be down even though a majority of the stocks can be up. The companies making up Dow 30 are also very large capitalized stocks. The beta is also very low in these large cap stocks. A stock with a beta of one will move dollar for dollar with the overall market. Even in volatile times these stocks can have a beta that is less than one.

A bottom up approach looks at individual securities first. If the 30 day EMA is pointing down and the indexes are pulling away from the 30 day EMA then it is a waste of time running bullish scans.

Weekend Work

Weekly charts should be looked at once a week. As a short term swing trader there is no need to look at weekly charts on a daily basis. Position trader who holds a position for several weeks or months only needs to glance at a weekly chart on the weekend. Even then your analysis should focus on the indexes and sector work.

Figure 8.1 is a weekly chart of the S&P 500 index showing a decline starting in October 2007 and the first rise off the March 2009 low of more than 20 percent. Is the rise off the bottom **the** low? It very well might be but it doesn't matter. It is tradable. The question is while this rise was happening what sectors should you have been looking at?

Figure 8.1

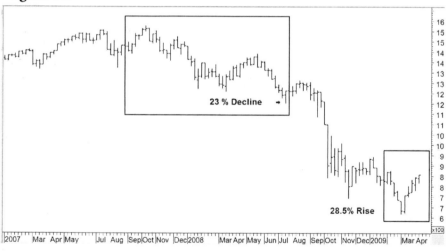

Charts powered by Metastock

Telechart[1] has a great feature that lets you sort a list of securities for a specified date range and put them in order based on the percentage move. This one feature makes Telechart an invaluable tool. A watchlist can be made up of Exchange Traded Funds of the major sectors that make up the S&P. The table in figure 8.2 are the ETF's I use.

Figure 8.2

XLY	Consumer Discretionary SPDR
XLP	Consumer Staples SPDR
XLE	Energy SPDR
XLF	Financials SPDR
XLV	Health Care SPDR
XLI	Industrials SPDR
XLB	Materials SPDR
XLK	Technology SPDR
XLU	Utilities SPDR

The Standard and Poor's Company breaks down the S&P index into nine sectors adding telecom with the tech sector. They came up with the Select Sector SPDRs ETF's.[2]

The weekly chart of the S&P in figure 8.1 shows the all time high of the bull market made in the week of October 12, 2007. The table in figure 8.3 shows when the sector ETF's made their high.

Figure 8.3

XLF	June, 6, 2007
XLY	July, 12, 2007
XLI	October 12, 2007
S&P 500	October 12, 2007
XLK	November 2, 2007
XLU	December 17, 2007
XLV	December 17, 2007
XLB	May 27, 2008
XLE	May 27, 2008
XLP	September 25, 2008

---

2   Select Sector SPDRs are trademarks of the McGraw-Hill Companies, Inc.

The Financials (XLF) started the decline four months ahead of the S&P. Consumer Discretionary (XLY) soon followed. After all, sales of big ticket items are the first thing to slow down when the economy starts to slow. Energy and consumer staples held up the longest. It is not uncommon to see commodity stocks hold up the market. That thought is short lived.

The week of July 16, 2008 the S&P was down over 20 percent from its high officially being called a bear market. Consumer staples are considered a safe haven. The thinking is that everyone will still buy toothpaste. The XLP pushed higher for another ten weeks after the bear market has been called. That means that for another 50 trading days the public was still buying stocks pushing prices to new highs. In reality they do still buy toothpaste but now they have to sell their stock in Procter & Gamble (PG) to afford it.

Just like the stock of the year can often be the worst performer the following year, the sectors that lead the way down can become the new leaders in the next market upturn.

The table in figure 8.4 shows the weekly advance of the nine ETF's. They are listed in order from the strongest sector to the weakest after a six consecutive week rally in the S&P.

Figure 8.4

Week	3/5—3/12	3/5—3/19	3/5—3/26	3/5—4/2	3/5—4/9	3/5—4/17
XLF	30.45	38.78	51.12	49.20	70.35	78.04
XLY	10.42	16.68	26.61	29.43	34.33	38.50
XLI	9.89	15.87	25.40	26.68	30.70	34.72
XLB	11.5	19.21	28.84	29.39	31.21	34.56
S&P	9.99	14.87	22.02	22.24	25.49	27.40
XLK	8.25	13.03	19.07	21.35	23.20	24.89
XLE	9.15	17.23	19.44	17.64	18.84	19.31
XLP	3.10	6.31	11.04	11.50	10.28	12.61
XLU	.39	11.20	12.28	11.93	12.32	12.42
XLV	6.28	7.83	11.61	10.61	9.83	11.20

It is not a coincidence that the first to fall was the first to rally. It is uncanny that the three sectors happen to rally in the exact order that they fell. This is why it's a bad idea to have a favorite stock. Banks are not usually considered a "Wall Street darling". That title is usually reserved for high flying tech stocks. But when the rally started, it started with the Financials. The rally was so strong the media could not even talk the banks down. Many "Wall Street experts" publicly said that it was too early to invest in the banks. The reality is that the financials beat the S&P three fold. You as a technician knew that after the first week. Every weekend after that your weekends work confirmed this.

This is not to say that you put all of your money into the financial sector. This just means that you wanted to be overweight the financials during this six week rally. You also want to stay away from sectors that are grossly underperforming the major indexes.

Sorting the S&P 500 and the NASDAQ 100 indexes from the week the low was made through the end of the current week will also show you the new market leaders. I cannot express the importance of this. If you are looking to go long, then you want to be in the strongest stocks. Don't pick a stock from the middle of the pile thinking you can get it at a good price and it will catch up. You get what you pay for. I have made this mistake and paid the price. When you zoom in on a chart it looks like the stock has made a huge run and you missed it. The thinking is that the fourth or fifth best hasn't made the move yet and it's due. Just suppose you had the opportunity to bet on a horse race after it had already started and the horses were just rounding the turn to the final stretch. They just start to pour it on. Would you step up to the window and bet on a horse from the end of the pack thinking it can catch up? Of course you wouldn't. Remember, you are not investing for the long haul. You are trading. You are not looking to pick the bottom or the top. You are just looking to take a small piece out of the middle. You want to go long the strongest stocks and short the weakest.

You should also compare the chart of the NASDAQ to the S&P 500. The NASDAQ is made up of much smaller capitalized companies. Figure 8.5 shows a weekly chart of the NASDAQ. It has rallied almost 28 percent from the low made in early March. This is less than one percent different from the S&P for the same time period. The only difference is that the NASDAQ is through the overhead resistance. This is a very important fact to make note of.

Figure 8.5

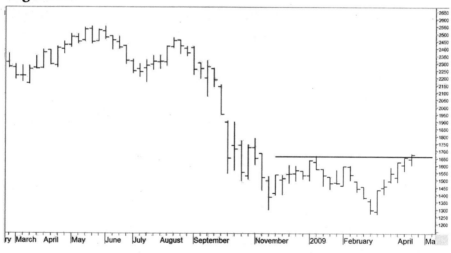

Charts powered by Metastock

Follow through to the upside will give strong support at the 1665 level. What was once resistance will now become support. The longer this support will hold the more the odds improve that the bottom is in.

Nightly Work

At the end of every day while your data is downloading you should check your bottom line. Investors look at quarterly statements. As a trader you should keep an eye on your bottom line daily. Your objective should be to make a profit on a weekly basis.

The first thing you should look at is the daily charts of the S&P and the NASDAQ. By looking at the charts of the indexes first it gives you a chance to get an un-influenced opinion on the market. If you look at charts of your positions first you might try to see something that is not there. Maybe your stock still is in an uptrend but if the indexes give a sell signal then you should get out or at the very least tighten your stops.

Figure 8.6

Charts powered by Metastock

A look at figure 8.6 shows the daily chart of the S&P. At point **A** the S&P breaks above the 30 day EMA. This in itself is not a signal to go long. Point **B** is a test of the 30 day EMA. Notice how the moving average holds. At this point you should have already had sectors and stocks on your watchlist from your weekend work. At point **C** you have confirmation when the high at bar **B** is broken. At this point the 30 day EMA has turned up. Orders can be placed to go long.

We know from our weekend work that at this point the financials, materials and consumer discretionary stocks are leading the way. We now run our scans looking for bullish setups.

Scans don't have to be something magical. You are still going to have to look through hundreds of charts. As you get more experienced this process will go quick. In the first go round you don't need to spend more than a few seconds looking at a chart.

Here is the process when looking to go long:

1. You want to scan for stocks trading above the 30 day EMA and the 10 day SMA above the 30 day EMA. The average daily volume should be at least 500,000 shares a day. You should also set a minimum price. Usually $10 a share. (In the beginning of 2009 six of the Dow 30 stocks hit single digits. You can adjust in extreme market conditions).

2. Depending on your software program you should scan for stocks making a pullback. Whether you use a proprietary scan or just sort the list based on a 5 period RSI. The sort should be in order with the lower value at the top of the list. Higher values show overbought conditions. You need to keep the RSI parameters set to a minimum of 3 and a maximum of 5. We are not looking for major pullbacks.

3. Flip through the charts quickly looking for strong up trends that are pulling back. Also look for stocks breaking out of a base. Gap-pause trades are some of the most profitable. Make a list of possible candidates.

4. Double check the list and cross out any stocks that happen to be in a weak sector.

5. At this point the list should be much smaller. Go back and revisit the charts. Look for overhead resistance. The resistance can be in the form of a major moving average, former support now overhead resistance or an old high. It could also be in the form of a Fibonacci line. If resistance is only a few points away, cross it off your list.

6. You should now have a short list. If you have several stocks from the same sector, pick the strongest.

7. Check to make sure earnings are not due to be released within the next few days. Buying a day or two before earnings is gambling.

8. Look where the stop will have to be set. If one stock allows a technical stop and another stock requires a dollar stop due to a wide range bar, then go with the technical stop all else being equal.

9. Place your buy order along with the stop order.

Let's look at some examples. Figure 8.7 is a chart of Dupont (DD). Dupont is a chemical company. We know from our weekend work that the materials are out pacing the S&P. On the second day of the pullback the low broke through the 10 day SMA and closed well off the low. An order to enter the market is placed above the prior bar's high at point **A**. Your stop is below the signal bar at point **B** and the first profit target is at point **C**.

Figure 8.7

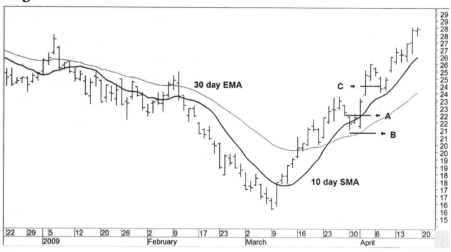

Charts powered by Metastock

Most brokers of late let you place oco (one cancels other) and first order triggers oco orders. Here is how your order should be placed.

#1 Order Description   Buy 300 DD 22.52 stop

#2 Order Description   Sell 300 DD 21.41 stop triggered by #1 oco

#3 Order Description   Sell 200 DD 24.50 limit triggered by #1 oco

Based on our $20,000 account we used in the example in chapter 7 we would look to risk 2 percent or $400 on this trade. Risking 4 percent would allow us to buy 444 shares. A 5 percent risk would put us with a well placed technical stop. So we go with the 5 percent stop and lower the size to 300 shares. Upon our order being filled, our stop loss is set to sell out all 300 shares for a 5 percent loss. You must always keep it in the back of your mind that an overnight gap to the downside could occur increasing the loss beyond 5 percent. Sooner or later this will happen.

The third order is your profit order. Notice that all 300 shares have a stop loss but only 200 shares have a profit target. If you are wrong on the trade, you are out all 300 shares and you move on. If the stock rallies you pick up $2 a share or almost 9 percent. (As a rule you look to sell one half to two thirds at the first profit target). If this happens, your protective stop is cancelled by the oco order. You need to do this because you now only have 100 shares to protect. You then place a stop loss order at the breakeven price of $22.52. As the stock moves up, you trail the stop in hopes of picking up a larger percentage profit on the remaining shares. As long as the stock does not gap down, you are getting out even (less commissions).

How you trail your stop depends on how aggressive you want to be. If the market is very over bought or showing signs of weakness, you might want to place your stop under the two day low. If all looks good, you could place your stop under the 10 day SMA. Your stop would be moved daily. Notice on the example of DD that a two bar low would have stopped you out around the $24.75 area. With the 10 day SMA stop you would still be in the market.

Why wait for Confirmation?

There is always a debate as to whether you should enter with a buy stop or just buy at the market and get a better price. The thought is that if you get a better price your stop will be lower increasing your chance of staying in the trade.

Once you see a two bar pullback you place your buy stop above the trigger high. If the stock resumes its uptrend you then get sucked into the market. This order is only a day order. If you do not get filled and the stock makes a lower high the third day, you then move your buy stop lower over that day's high. You are awaiting confirmation that the stock is going to resume its uptrend. Unless market conditions change, you can place a buy stop for up to five bars from the reaction high. If after five days into the pullback the stock does not resume its trend you move on. The stock might be at an inflection point. Figure 8.8 is a daily chart of Diamond Offshore Drilling (DO). DO was running strong for six weeks gaining almost 40 percent. Three bars into the pullback and the $142 level held. Point **A** is where the buy stop should be. The next day was a lower low and a lower high. The 10 day SMA held and DO still looks like a buy. The buy stop should be placed at point **B**. The fifth day off the high and DO still looks like a buy. This stock has not done anything wrong technically. The trend line drawn from the lows made at the end of November to the lows at the end of December shows that the stock is still holding up. The 10 day SMA is sloping up and the ADX still has a reading of 36. Any reading over 30 is considered a strong trend. This is the last day to try to enter a position in DO. A buy stop should be placed at point **C**. Price tells all and the fact that DO cannot break its prior day's high after five consecutive days should tell you to move on.

Figure 8.8

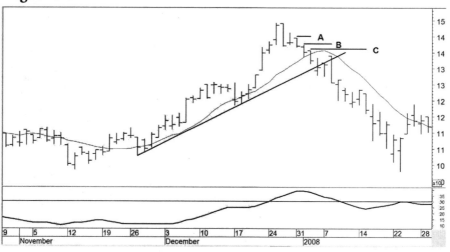

Charts powered by Metastock

By waiting for confirmation you stayed out of a trade that would have gone bad. Also by waiting for confirmation you know where support is. If you got filled at point **B** then you know the low of the trigger bar is support. Remember, the bars on a chart represent people. The low is where buyers stepped in to support the stock. If they supported it once, the odds are in your favor that they will support it again. Just because you decided to jump in anywhere doesn't mean other traders will do the same.

Let's look at one more example.

Figure 8.9

Charts powered by Metastock

Target (TGT) made a two bar pullback and bounced off its 10 day SMA. Notice how it also closed in the upper 25 percent of the day's range. A buy stop should be placed at point **A** for $33.62. Using our $20,000 account the order would go as follows:

#1 Order Description   Buy 300 TGT 33.62 stop

#2 Order Description   Sell 300 TGT 32.46 stop triggered by #1 oco

#3 Order Description   Sell 200 TGT 36.00 limit triggered by #1 oco

Although the stock price is higher than the example of DD in figure 8.7 you can still trade 300 shares due to the stop being less that 4 percent away. The stop on the remaining 100 shares should be trailed. Notice the two bar low also broke through the 10 day SMA intraday. If market conditions are in your favor a looser stop will keep you in the trade longer. Take note how stocks in a strong uptrend just penetrate the 10 day SMA intraday. Give a little room below the average if you use that as a stop.

The Playbook

Not having access to a computer throughout the day is going to require you to keep a playbook. A small spiral bound notebook that will fit into your pocket is ideal. You will need to keep an updated list of your positions along with the size and your current stop.

It should read as follows:

AAPL long 200 shares @ 105.50 trailing stop @ 115.66

BIDU May 180 call 1 @ 18.10 stop BIDU< 199

You also need to keep a list of orders you have placed or orders you might be placing that day. You need to document all important information in case you need to adjust your orders.

Your hit list should read as follows:

WFT buy 500 @ 14.62 stop yesterday's low – 13.43 high – 14.52

10 SMA – 13.35 20 EMA – 12.90 pivot high 14.92

Checking on the market throughout the day on your wireless device can offer some benefits. A perfect example would be if you checked on the market at 10:00 and found the market running strong and WFT opened down at 13.32 and was currently trading at 14.50. Even without looking at a chart you know that WFT had an opening gap reversal. It opened at the 10 day SMA and it held. WFT then went to close the gap and is now within the prior days range. With the rest of the market up you can cancel your buy stop and enter at the market and get in 12 cents lower with a well defined stop.

Keeping a playbook can really come in handy if you are able to get alerts on your wireless device. If you are looking to trade options on the stock you can list the option strike and symbol you are looking to trade. You then set an alert just below your trigger price. This will often give you time to log on to your account. If the stock triggers, you can place your buy order for your option. Unless the option is heavily traded like a front month option in a stock like Caterpillar (CAT) you can get beat up on a market order with a large spread. I have seen Google (GOOG) have a $100 spread between the bid and the ask in a front month option. You can often split the bid and the ask and get a much better price than you would with a market order.

A journal should also be kept for every trade made. Looking back on the journal entries will help you become a better trader. Examining your losing trades is probably more important than your winning trades. At the back of this manual is what a typical journal entry should look like.

Sideways Markets

Position traders and most momentum traders hate sideways markets. Position traders are sitting on dead money and momentum traders find themselves getting whipsawed.

While many die hard momentum traders sit on their hands for what could be months, I like to take the U.S. Marine Corps approach. That is to "Improvise, Adapt and Overcome." You will not hit any homeruns but your risk - reward is very good. Your percentage of winning trades will also be very high.

This is where a playbook will really come in handy. You can flip through your charts on the weekend and come up with a list of stocks that are range bound. From there you list the buy point and the sell point. As the stock is building a base you can trade in one or both directions. If the market is extremely oversold, you might look to trade just on the long side until the market gives you a clue as to where it might be heading next. A very nimble trader can trade from both sides.

Figure 8.10

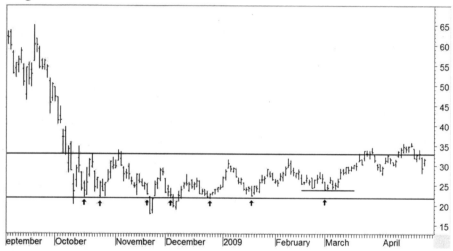

Charts powered by Metastock

The chart of National Oilwell Varco in figure 8.10 was range bound for six months before it broke out to the upside. The range was established in October between $21.85 and $32.85. That 11 point range is a 50 percent move. Notice at the end of November, early December support was broken and bounced back the next day. If you did happen to get long on these pullbacks you would have got stopped out for a small loss. The win/loss ratio would more than make up for this.

Here is how the trade works:

1. You find stocks that are range bound that have at least $5 or more between the high and low.

2. Record them in your playbook. If there are intermediate highs and lows, make note of them.

3. Place a limit order to buy near the low.

4. Once filled place a stop order (just below support) oco sell (just below resistance) limit.

Let's take a look at one more example. In figure 8.11 Chesapeake Energy (CHK) had a range between $13.40 and $19.15. That is a $5.75 range or 43 percent. A perfect candidate. You don't draw the lines at the extremes but rather at points hit more often. Use the hourly charts supplied by your broker to help determine this price range. The range really was not established until point **A**. CHK could have been bought with a limit order 50 cents above support and a stop order should be placed 50 cents below support. In this example you would be looking for 4 points. 4:1 risk – reward is not bad. At point **B** the range is more defined. Notice how you had several days where you could have gotten in.

Figure 8.11

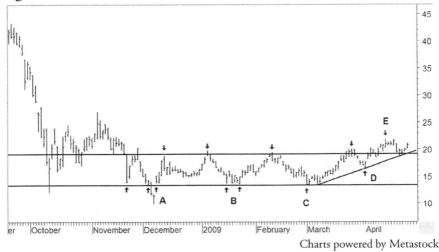

Charts powered by Metastock

When you get out you sell the whole position. Yes there will eventually be a breakout to one side or the other. If you notice there are about 10 trading days between the highs and the lows. You don't have that much time. By selling only half and using a trailing stop you might only get 2 points for the remainder of your position. That brings the risk – reward down to 2:1. Remember we are not looking for homeruns. We are just looking to keep hitting singles.

After the trade at point **C** you would have gotten out again at the $19 level only to see CHK break through resistance. It never came back to the $13 level. CHK hit a low of 16.68 and rallied to make a higher high. Now you draw a trend line and watch it. The difference between point **D** and point **E** is 5.19. So if you bought the next time CHK hit the trend line at $18.70, you would look to get out around $23.40. That is the trend line plus $5.19 minus 50 cents.

One more important point to make when trading range bound stocks. Market makers look to take you out. That's why many traders use mental stops. They don't want the market makers to know ahead of time where their stop is. Other people are making the same trades. You need to beat them to the punch. If a stock keeps making highs at $19.25 then other traders are looking to get out at the $19.25 level. All that selling will bring the price down. So what you do is look to sell at an odd number. Try putting your limit order in at $19.22. The same goes for your stop order. A stop order to sell at $12.96 is less likely to get hit than a stop order of $13.00. If the stock is thinly traded your stop might still get hit. What you can do to stop this from happening is place a contingent order with your broker. It would read as a market order continent upon the last trade being $12.96. This way the trade is not placed with the market maker until the condition is met. You will have more slippage but you will stay in the game where many times you might have been taken out when a market maker runs stops

Rules to Never Break

1. **Always use a stop loss.** Preservation of capital is second to nothing. Break this rule and you will not succeed as trader.

2. **Never average down.** If a trade starts to go against you that means you are wrong. Why be more wrong? Wait until your stop is hit and you are out or wait until you are showing a profit if you want to add to the position.

3. **Never trade against the trend.** You will put the odds gravely against you if you ignore this one rule.

4. **Never let a profit turn into a loss.** Always move your stop to break even once a reasonable profit is realized.

5. **Don't over leverage.** The use of options is to limit risk and lessen the cost of a trade so one can be more diversified. Options should not be used to over leverage.

6. **Only trade in active stocks.** I thought this was worth mentioning because so many times people ask me my opinion about a stock just to find out its some penny stock that trades 100,000 shares a day. Stay away. Don't try to discover the next Microsoft.

7. **Ignore the media.** I have lost more money listening to the financial gurus than I have on my own. More times than I would like to count, I cashed in positions because I second guessed myself. I heard some "expert" on TV say to dump a stock because earning were going to be bad just to watch it open 20 percent higher in the next day or two.

8. **Never increase your size after a winning streak.** After a hot streak you should cash out of most of your positions or at the very least, tighten your stops. Two months of gains can be given back in a couple of weeks.

9. **Always have a good reason to enter a trade.** Don't buy just because you think the stock is priced cheap. It can always get cheaper.

10. **Don't have a favorite stock.** A favorite stock should be one that is making you money right now. Once you are out, move on. Don't stalk a stock looking for a setup that is not there.

11. **Don't over trade.** If the reason you entered a trade has not changed and you haven't been stopped out. Let the trade go on. If after a week or so goes by and the stock is still flat. Then call it "dead money" and move on.

12. **Never hope or wish.** Save your hopes and wishes for blowing out birthday candles. There is no place for them in the market.

13. **Never chase a stock.** If you missed the setup, then you missed the setup. Move on.

14. **Never let a trade turn into an investment.** Doing so would break rule number one.

15. **Never buy spontaneously.** A stock on the active list should not be bought without research. Always look at the punch list. Market, sector, weekly then daily charts. Decisions made during market hours are based more on emotion than decisions made after the market has closed.

16. **Never feel that a stock owes you.** If you had a loss in a stock, move on. Don't try to get your money back from a stock.

17. **Don't sell covered calls or hedge.** We are not investing. We are trading. Selling a covered call will keep you married to a stock.

18. **Never get out unless you have good reason.** Unless something has changed since you entered the trade, let it work.

19. **Have a time stop.** Some people will argue this rule. If you entered a trade and momentum dies and the stock starts trading sideways, get out. It has become dead money that could be used elsewhere. This goes especially true for option trades.

20. **Never ever break rule number one.**

Chapter 9

Appendix

Glossary

Accumulation – When a stock is building a base, institutional traders quietly buy in small amounts to build their position slowly.

At The Money (ATM) – An option that has the same strike price as the underlying stock.

Base – When price moves in a very narrow range for an extended period of time. Traders look for a breakout to the upside from a base.

Bear trap – A downside breakout that lures traders into selling short only to be met with a quick price reversal to the upside.

Bearish Divergence – When price makes a higher high and a momentum indicator does not.

Beta- A measurement of volatility showing how much the price of a stock moves compared to the index (S&P). A stock with a beta less than one means that for every one percent the index moves the stock moves less than one percent. A high beta stock (like a tech stock) can have a beta of 2.

Bull trap – An upside breakout that lures traders into buying only to be met with a quick price reversal to the downside.

Bullish Divergence – When price makes a lower low and a momentum indicator does not.

Capitulation – A sign of a bottom when there is heavy selling on high volume. It is believed that there is no one left to sell and bargain hunters step up to buy.

Counter Trend – A trade made in the opposite direction from the major trend.

Delta – A ratio comparing how much an option will move for every point in the underlying stock. An ATM option usually has a delta of .50 moving 50 cents for every dollar the stock moves.

Distribution – Institutional traders sell in small amounts so they don't drive the price down before they unload their whole position.

Fade the market – A high risk trade where a trader will buy when the market is falling and vice-versa. It is commonly used for opening gaps.

Head and shoulders – A price pattern in an uptrend where price makes a new high (left shoulder) and then pulls back and makes a higher high (Head). Price then pulls back once again but this time makes a lower high (right shoulder). It is a topping pattern. A break of the neckline (lows between shoulders and head) is a sign to sell short.

In The Money (ITM) – An option that has intrinsic value. Example: a call option with a strike price lower than the stock price.

Inside day – A day where the high is lower than the prior day's high and the low is higher than the prior day's low. In other words, the day's range is within the prior day's range.

Intrinsic value – The dollar amount of an option that is in the money. Its real value

Market Breath – How many stocks are up vs. how many stocks are down on the NYSE.

Narrow range bar – A bar where the difference between the high and low is very minimal.

Out of The Money (OTM) – An option that has no intrinsic value. Example: a call option with a strike price high than the stock price.

Pivot point – A peak or trough on a chart. Breaking through a pivot point can show confirmation of a trend or show a trend reversal.

Relative Strength Index (RSI) – A momentum indicator developed by Welles Wilder. A reading over 70 is considered over bought and a reading under 30 is considered over sold.

Slippage – When an order gets filled at a different price than the expected price because of market conditions.

Wide range bar – A price bar that has a range far greater than the preceding bars.

Journal

Entry

Stock_____ Long____ Short____ Date in_____

Option_____ Price_____ Size_____

Stop_____

Pattern_____

Notes_____

_____

_____

_____

S&P _____

NASDQ_____

Sector_____

Deviation from plan _____

_____

_____

_____

Exit

First exit_____ Date_____

Second exit_____ Date_____

profit/loss _____

Dissection of Trade

_____

_____

_____

_____

_____

Must Read List

I thought long and hard as to what books I would be listing here. I must have read at least one hundred books on trading ranging in price from $10 to $175. The more expensive books are supposed to contain someone's trading secrets. They're not for me.

You read reviews on the web and it seems people are always getting ticked when they buy a book and the secret that is going to make them a millionaire overnight isn't between the covers of the book. I'll save you a lot of time and money by saying that book is not out there. Take each book for what it's worth and try to learn one tip or benefit from someone else's insight.

Below is a list of books that you will find yourself rereading and referring back to from time to time. There are many other good books out there. These are just a few of my favorites.

Reminiscence of a Stock Operator
By Edwin Lefé'vre
What a great story. I never could have imagined that a book on the life story of Jesse Livermore would add so much to my trading. To be a great trader, you need to think like a great trader. This book gives insight to Livermore's view of the markets.

How to trade in Stocks
By Jesse Livermore with updates by Richard Smitten
To say this book is great is an understatement. If you are looking for that Holy Grail that made Livermore his millions, you will not find it here, (or anywhere for that matter). What this book will do for you is give you a look into the mind and the way a legendary trader thinks.

Dave Landry on Swing Trading
By Dave Landry
Dave has done so much to help educate new traders. His first book gets the new swing traders' feet wet. It also has plenty of material for the more advanced trader.

Dave Landry's 10 Best Swing Trading Patterns and Strategies
By Dave Landry
In Dave's second book on swing trading, Dave gets even more back to basics. His theories and setups are based strictly on price action.

How I Made $2,000,000 In The Stock Market
By Nicolas Darvas
Darvas was a dancer who entered the market without any knowledge of the markets and learned the hard way. By losing his hard earned money. He then proceeded to turn $10,000 into $2 million in just 18 months. He was a buy high and sell higher kind of guy. His system was an earlier version of William O'Neil's (founder of Investors Business Daily) CANSLIM system.

Technical Analysis of the Financial Markets
By John Murphy
This is the bible of technical analysis. Every trader's book shelf is not complete without a copy. You will find yourself referring back to this book regularly. It covers everything from Gann to Elliot. Point and figure, candlesticks and even covers the futures market.

Market Wizards
By Jack Schwager
Jack Schwager is a genius for coming up with the idea for this book. A must read

The New Market Wizards
By Jack Schwager
This book picks up where the Market Wizards left off.

Bibliography

CNBC.com. "Bear Sterns CEO: No Liquidity Crisis for Firm"
http://www.cnbc.com/id/23630492 copyright 2009

Reuters. "TIMELINE: A dozen key dates in the demise of Bear
Stearns"
http://www.reuters.com/article/newsOne/idUSN1724031920080317
copyright March. 17, 2008

Banking, Housing, & Urban Affairs. Statement of Alan Schwartz
http://banking.senate.gov/public/_files/SchwartzStmt4308.pdf
April 3, 2008

Jesse Livermore with added material by Richard Smitten. "How To
Trade in Stocks". Copyright 2001 by Richard Smitten

INDEX